New Life Clarity Publishing

205 West 300 South, Brigham City, Utah 84302
Http://newlifeclarity.com/

The Right of Kelly Kaye Walker to be identified as the Author of the work has been asserted by her in accordance with the Copyright Act 1988.

New Life Clarity Publishing
name has been established by NLCP.
All Rights Reserved.

No part of this publication may be reproduced, distributed, or transmitted in any form or by any means, including photocopying, recording, or other electronic or mechanical methods without the prior and express written permission of the author or publisher, except in the case of brief quotations embodied in critical reviews and certain other noncommercial uses permitted by copyright law.

Printed in the United States of America
ISBN- 9780578776149
Copyright@2020 Kelly Kaye Walker

The Drive-Thru Method of Manifesting

The 6-Step Formula to Get Anything You Want

KELLY KAYE WALKER

Dedication

To my sweet, endlessly patient, supportive, husband who cheered me on, took on extra responsibilities, and regularly let me make terrifyingly (at the time) large purchases of coaching programs to go from the depressed, checked-out-of-life mess I was 4 years ago to the completely different woman I am today.

Thank you, Lynn. I love you.

Foreword by Jennifer Bryce Seely

I first met Kelly about a year ago. She was speaking to a group of female entrepreneurs and told the delightful story you'll read about in Chapter 11, complete with toilet noises. I signed up for her free audit and joined her amazing Facebook group (called "Manifesting Influence, Clients, and Purpose"). I was part of the first group ever to take her Manifesting Clients class, because it was the wish list I had for all the things I needed to learn in my business. And I wasn't disappointed. I still refer to those course materials as I work toward my goals.

Honestly, she spoiled us all for any other coach out there. She is generous, kind, forgiving, patient, and knowledgeable. In the time I've been working with Kelly (in two more courses and her advanced Manifesting group), I've grown tremendously. Using the manifesting formula, the belief breakthrough process, and her accountability tracker has helped me to achieve some amazing goals.

But you know what I find the most amazing about Kelly? It was the day she turned to me for my help. I didn't think coaches did that. They know it all, don't they? I have come to realize that all the good coaches have their own coaches, because they know the value of the coaching process. They're all learning and giving and learning some more and giving some more. But the coach who can turn around and learn from a student is something even more special and magnificent and beautiful.

And that's what Kelly's book is. She is giving you an incredible gift in this book. Far more than "shifting your mindset", far more than "raising your vibration", far more than "leaning in", this book is personal, one-on-one, go-at-your-own pace coaching. Her step-by-step, practical application process can guide anyone through the process of becoming who you're really meant to be.

Enjoy the blessings that are coming your way!

Table of Contents

1 The Key to Manifesting 1
2 Your Thoughts Matter 7
3 How I Learned to Manifest 17
4 What You Focus On Grows 27
5 Manifesting in Alignment With Your Purpose 39
6 Step #1: Clarification 49
7 Step #2: Visualization 59
8 Step #3: Declaration 79
9 Step #4: Meditation 95
10 Step #5: Inspiration 103
11 Step #6: Implementation 111
12 Speed Manifesting 125
13 Stretching Your Comfort Zone 131
14 Vibrational Frequency Affects Everything 139
15 Troubleshooting 149
16 What's Next? 157

Introduction

My name is Kelly Walker and I am the Queen of Manifesting, which means that I know how to get what I want.

Disclaimer: I don't always get what I want.

I don't want you to think that you have to be perfect at manifesting to get what you want. Even after successfully manifesting so many things I once thought impossible, I still accidentally manifest the things I worry about. Even I don't always consistently follow all the steps I'm going to teach you in this book. I'm still working on my own thoughts and consistency too!

However, I do know that the more closely you stick to the formula, the faster and easier you will manifest your goals. Just don't get caught up in 'perfect.' Perfectionism leads to self-judgment, frustration, and giving up. Grant yourself the gift of grace—we all make mistakes and we can all pick ourselves up, find the help we need, and move forward with confidence.

Let yourself fall short, screw up, have a tantrum, and anything else that comes with being human, but then use this book to figure it out. Keep trying. Get back up when you fall. You will get better and better at manifesting as you practice. I know it's totally cliché, but if I can do it, YOU absolutely can do it

CLARIFICATION:
FIGURE OUT WHAT YOU WANT.

VISUALIZATION:
SEE YOURSELF WITH IT.

DECLARATION:
SPEAK IT OUT LOUD.

MEDITATION:
CLEAR YOUR DISTRACTIONS.

INSPIRATION:
RECEIVE AN INSPIRED NEXT STEP.

IMPLEMENTATION:
TAKE THAT STEP IMMEDIATELY.

The Manifesting Formula

I used to try to explain manifesting by saying 'change your thoughts, change your words, change your outcomes.' But I could tell that people didn't really 'get it' with that explanation. Then I came up with my very well-researched (and even rhyming) six step formula to manifesting. While it made perfect sense in my head, I could see that I still wasn't creating the a-ha moment I was hoping for on a regular basis.

And then one day in October 2019, it occurred to me that the process of ordering food from a drive-thru window was nearly identical to my manifesting formula. Suddenly I had an explanation that everyone could understand. When I started using the drive-thru metaphor in my presentations, I started to see light bulbs going off all through the audience and realized I had powerful imagery to illustrate the process of manifesting better than anything I had tried before.

I was so excited that I had been given the perfect way to teach manifesting that I decided it was time to write this book. It has been rattling around in the back of my head for at least a year, refusing to solidify into the recognizable form of a book, until now.

This book has all the ins and outs of manifesting that I have learned, misapplied, discovered, misunderstood, figured out, and experienced personally. I have failed at, tweaked, succeeded at and refined the process, and watched others use

The Drive-Thru Method of Manifesting as effectively as I have been able to.

I am going to give you all the detailed explanations of each step later, but I know that there are lots of you who want to hurry and get manifesting right now! So, for those of you that want to skip the details and get right to the point (before you get distracted by something else and forget what you were doing) here it is:

The Drive-Thru Method of Manifesting.

Clarification:
Figure out what you want. Get so clear that you can talk about it for 30 minutes straight. Drive-thru equivalent? Choosing which restaurant's drive-thru you want to go through and order food from.

Visualization:
See it in as much detail as possible as if you are living it. Drive-thru equivalent? Look at the menu and see the pictures of the food you want to eat and imagine yourself eating it.

Declaration:
Speak your desires out loud. Words have power! Drive-thru equivalent? Lean out your window and speak your order out loud. You have to say it loud or you get no food.

Meditation:
Stop the noise and distraction for a few minutes to clear your mind and make room for inspiration. Drive-thru equivalent? Sit in your car with your window rolled down, the radio off, and just be silent.

Inspiration:
Receive inspiration telling you your next step. Drive-thru equivalent? Hear what the voice coming out of the speaker tells you to do next so you know how to get your food.

Implementation:
Act immediately on whatever inspiration comes to you. Drive-thru equivalent? Do whatever the voice says in order to collect your food. Or else you get no food!

That's it! Simple enough, right? For sure. But simple does not always mean easy. I will make it as easy for you as I can so you can finally achieve success in all those goals you have been working on over the years (and maybe even decades).

Let me remind you, like I said earlier, I am not perfect at manifesting on purpose all the time. I get distracted easily. Focusing my mental energy is a little hard for me to do for more than a minute or two. I scored off the charts when I was tested for ADHD in my 40s and subsequently finally understood why I seem to have the attention span of a squirrel. I have to work extra hard at focusing my mental energy and

I don't want you to think it's something that's super easy for others while you struggle with it.

Most of us have short attention spans. And they are getting shorter all the time. Spending time each day actively thinking about and talking about your goals can be like learning a new language - you have to form new neural pathways in your brain and build up your endurance for focusing on something longer than you ever have before. So please don't judge yourself to be bad at manifesting if you struggle at first. Keep trying. Keep practicing. You can do it. This book will save you YEARS of struggling through the long painful part of wondering why you keep creating every situation you worry about.

You will learn how to manifest on purpose when you read this book, but you are still going to be human. On purpose, you ask? Yes. All of us are manifesting all the time, but we are doing it by accident and like so many accidents, the results are not usually pleasant. We manifest on accident anytime we feel an intense emotion about something. And unfortunately, most of our strongest emotions are negative - like fear, anger, jealousy, frustration and grief. They also tend to last longer than the intense positive emotions, which makes the negative ones much more likely to cause something to manifest in your life.

Manifesting on accident is something everyone does every day - and it's almost always manifesting the things you hope don't happen. Learning how to manifest on purpose instead of on accident is mind-blowingly powerful. You will have a huge advantage by skipping that whole nasty, unpleasant part of the process where you discover that your manifesting powers are nearly all being spent on your fears and worries!

Who wants to keep manifesting more of the things they intensely dislike or fear? Manifesting on accident can be extremely painful and cause you to feel powerless, which is completely false. You are more powerful than you can even imagine. Knowing how to manifest on purpose will not change you into a new person, but it will give you a glimpse into how powerful you truly are, and how you are absolutely 100% in control of your life. It will be an amazing tool in your tool belt that you will be able to pull out and use whenever you need it.

Manifesting on purpose takes a lot of mental energy and a lot of self-trust, which don't always come naturally. They definitely don't come naturally to me. But now when I decide to put my mental energy into achieving something I want, it happens. And when you decide to put your mental energy into getting what YOU want, it will happen for you, too.

Throughout this book you will find some of my Facebook or Blog posts that either illustrate a point of the manifesting formula or show examples of it as I gradually came to understand each principle of the formula along my journey.

THOUGHTS ARE
THINGS;
WHAT YOU FEEL,
YOU ATTRACT;
AND WHAT YOU
IMAGINE,
YOU BECOME.
—
JOSEPH MURPHY

Chapter 1

The Key to Manifesting

When I was much younger (and mistakenly assumed that I was much wiser that I actually was), I read *The Secret* by Rhonda Byrne. It was all about the Law of Attraction and how to use it.

My mind was blown. I felt like I had discovered a buried treasure chest full of gold coins and precious gems, the secrets to the universe, and my very own private wishing well, all rolled up into one!

Upon finishing the book, I went to bed with a plan. I was going to reshape my eyeballs while I slept that night and wake up with no more need for glasses, just like the author of The Secret had done. Surely I had as much enthusiasm and faith as was needed to do something so small as reshape my eyeballs for perfect 20/20 vision!

As I lay in bed that night, I thought about how I had wanted to have perfect vision for years. Going swimming was so unfair because I had to leave my glasses off, somewhere on the side of the pool, which meant I couldn't see anything but blurry blobs, never knowing where my friends were because I couldn't make out faces.

Kelly Kaye Walker

Every winter when I would enter a building from the freezing Kansas air outside, my glasses would instantly fog over and I would be blinded for at least a minute. Sometimes when I had to take them off for a shower or to go to bed, I would forget where I put them. Then I would have to ask for help from my family or roommates to find them for me, hoping earnestly that nobody would step on them in the search.

And, to my constant embarrassment, I had such bad vision, I always had to wear glasses so thick that they looked horrendous and weighed a ton! Any cute frame was totally ruined by the hideously thick lenses, no matter how stylish they looked with those skinny demo lenses.

But it was ok now, because I had just learned the secret to perfect vision. I just had to focus really hard on it like they said in the book! I went to bed that night thinking about how amazing it would be not to have to wear glasses. How awesome I would feel without glasses. How much better I would look without glasses. How much easier life would be without glasses.

Do you see the problem yet?

Every thought I had that night was about hating my glasses. Every emotion was negative. I focused entirely on how much I disliked wearing glasses!

Now I am not claiming that I could have just casually reshaped my eyeballs in one night if only I had done it right. I believe I could actually get perfect vision now if I bent all my will and manifesting energy into that goal, but I know it would take much longer than one night and it's just not that important to me anymore. I discovered ultra light lenses and now my glasses are one of my favorite things. The point is that I wasted all my concentration that night on the wrong thing - the thing I didn't want.

I woke up the next morning super excited to try out my new perfect vision. But when I opened my eyes, I was overcome with disappointment. Everything in my room was a blurry blob, just like normal. I realized that I, in fact, did not have the secret to perfect vision after all. I wondered what went wrong. Was it me? Was it something I did? Did I do it wrong? Was the book a hoax? Was the Law of Attraction a farce? Was I just a gullible fool? Looking back, I can laugh at my completely counterproductive way of attempting to manifest, but at the time I was crushed. And I am sure that I am not the only one who has felt powerless, stupid, not enough, or incapable of achieving goals.

What I didn't understand then is this: the key to manifesting is learning how to change your focus from what you fear, dislike, and worry about, to the things you actually want instead. Though the solution is simple, the implementation takes a lot of mental work that can seem confusing and difficult. But it doesn't have to be confusing or difficult.
Manifesting is the process by which you bring a person, thing or situation into your life through focusing significant mental

energy on it to the point that your thoughts, words and behaviors change. These changes work together to put you in the right places and the right times to make that thing you are focused on come to fruition in your life.

A common misconception of manifesting is the belief that you just have to wish really hard, and when you have finally wished hard for long enough, your goal will show up for you. Wishing is NOT the key. The key is believing with so much confidence that your goal/desire is already here that your thoughts, words, and actions shift in a way that cause your goal/desire to show up for you.

Notice the difference between true manifesting and the fake 'wishful thinking' type of manifesting - your thoughts, words and behaviors actually CHANGE. You think new thoughts. You speak different words. You take new action. The world doesn't change to create your new reality - YOU change your own reality by changing your perception of what's around you.

I am going to break it all down into easy-to-understand steps and give you explanations of what is happening in your conscious and subconscious mind along the way.

→ Now You Try It! ←

See how powerful you are at manifesting already. Scan through your life and write down a few times when you know, looking back at it now objectively, that you manifested something because you were so scared of it happening. Then do the same scan for a few times when you realize you manifested something because you were so excited about it and poured a ton of focus and energy into it.

TOO MANY OF US
ARE NOT LIVING
OUR DREAMS
BECAUSE WE ARE
LIVING OUR FEARS.
—
LES BROWN

Chapter 2

Your Thoughts Matter

I didn't always know how to manifest on purpose. In fact, I spent decades of my life being scared, powerless, worried, stuck, and depressed. Like most people, I was an expert at getting everything I didn't want.

That's because I didn't understand that I was manifesting all day, every day. Unfortunately, the raw materials I was feeding into my manifesting machine were negative emotions like fear, worry, anger and jealousy. From the outside, I looked like a semi-normal, happy person. I was loving, bossy, creative, impatient, smart, lazy, and funny. A pretty typical mix of personality traits.

But what people didn't see when they looked at me was the constant fear boiling just under the surface. I grew up in fear. I was always scared of something. Scared of incurring the wrath of an angry parent, scared of the dark, scared of being attacked by large dogs, scared of tornadoes, scared of my house burning down, scared of getting my wisdom teeth out, scared of boys doing things that confused me and made me uncomfortable, scared of saying "no" to anyone, scared of failure, scared of people judging me and finding me lacking, scared of looking stupid, scared of rejection.

Because I was always focused on the things I feared, scary things had to show up for me. They had no choice. One of the most basic explanations of manifesting is "What you focus on, grows." That explains why I spent most of my life accidentally manifesting all those things I was scared of experiencing.

And because everything I desperately tried to avoid always ended up happening anyway, I deduced early on that I had no control over the world. If everything I feared eventually came to pass, then I was a helpless victim to the cruel whims of the universe. **I believed at my core that I was powerless to change anything important to me.**

For years I worried that I would never get married. My subconscious mind knew that you can't get married if you never date anyone, so I ended up accidentally manifesting a complete lack of male interest. I went without a date for a decade, from age 18 to 28. Any boy I liked had no interest in me, which meant I was subconsciously choosing only boys that I energetically knew would reject me.

I was so scared of being an old maid that I nearly guaranteed it! Somehow God finally steered me to my husband in spite of my fear-induced anti-boy-manifesting and at age 28 I finally had a date, an engagement, and a husband by age 29. (I mention this because sometimes your manifesting can be thwarted completely by divine intervention, no matter how hard you fear something.)

A few years after getting married I became quite baby-hungry. Every Sunday at church I would see all the babies being held by adoring mom and dads, and I wanted nothing more than one of my own.

When we didn't get pregnant right away I got mildly worried. And as the negative pregnancy tests piled up, I developed a fear that I couldn't get pregnant at all.

Sundays became torture for me and I would often go home in tears. Whenever someone I knew announced they were pregnant again it ripped the barely formed scab off my heart and sent me into a sobbing fit.

I became obsessed with the fear of infertility. In fact, it became all I ever thought about after several failed fertility treatments.

After 8 years we gave up. I was reaching the age of dangerous, high risk pregnancies. I quit my very stressful job and we went to Mexico for a week. I stopped worrying about my infertility and had the time of my life. I came home to a new, much happier job and had little to no stress in my life.

And within a month I was pregnant. As soon as I stopped actively manifesting infertility, boom! Baby time!

Fast forward a few months and after a highly dangerous pregnancy we had an adorable baby boy. But then we had to deal with post-partum depression. We got it all figured out and then the depression took a turn for the worse about 10 years later. Medication didn't seem to help anymore and I felt like the depression was winning.

Then one day, out of the blue, right when I needed it most, I was offered a ticket to a three-day life-changing seminar. It was by email, from someone I barely knew. And as I sat there reading about the event, I thought "Wow, yeah, I could probably use some life changing."

As you can probably guess, some life changing definitely happened for me at that seminar. I learned the basics of manifesting and how I had been attracting all the bad things in my life.

It was then that I realized I had been manifesting by accident for years and years.

Everything I disliked about myself and my life had shown up because I had created it through fear, self-loathing, judgment, jealousy, and all the other negative emotions I kept on tap inside me.

I learned that if I wanted something different in my life, I just needed to start manifesting on purpose. The idea lit a spark in me that soon turned into a blazing bonfire. Over the next year I experienced a complete transformation. I learned how to manifest on purpose and create a life I am excited to wake up to in the morning.

I stopped hating myself. I stopped looking for evidence that I was a terrible wife and mom. I stopped telling myself mean things all day long in my head.

I started making goals. I thought about them with excitement. I came up with ideas for reaching those goals. I focused on my strengths, and how I could serve others.

I healed my relationships with my family, started my own business, became a coach, started speaking locally, then nationally, and now internationally.

My life is nearly unrecognizable from 4 years ago. And I couldn't be happier about the change.

My entire transformation can all be boiled down to the shift from manifesting on accident to manifesting on purpose.

As soon as I started focusing on what I wanted instead of what I feared and disliked, everything started to change. It was mind-bogglingly simple! Not necessarily easy, especially when you haven't had a lot of practice consciously focusing your thoughts. But so, so simple!

You can have a huge transformation like this too. Changing your focus from what you DON'T want to what you DO want is the basis for manifesting on purpose.

And that is what I'm going to teach you!

Kelly Kaye Walker

Facebook Post January 12, 2020

Three years ago today I was fired for the first time in my life and the burning shame I felt for weeks was almost unbearable.

I thought it was the low point of my adult life. Until the shame drove me to an addiction that fueled my shame to a whole new level. I became addicted to mind-numbing escape. I completely cut myself off from my family, sleeping all day and playing video games all night.

I couldn't face reality, because reality was full of pain, anger, abandonment and more shame. It didn't take long for me to start to plan something that would result in a permanent escape.

Shame is a powerful emotion that seems to multiply. As it grows, it invites all the other destructive emotions to move in.

Thankfully I chickened out on my plans and decided to stay here and suffer. Though it felt like the worst thing ever, those months of inner hell were the catalyst I needed to find out who I really was.

If I had not been fired, I would not have accepted that invitation to a 3 day seminar that taught me to see the first tiny glimpse of who I might really be.

I would have ignored that invitation, thinking I couldn't take off work, and that my life wasn't really bad enough for a "life-changing" seminar. I now thank my old boss every time I see him and give him a huge hug for 'kicking me out of the nest' so I could discover I have wings.

In the last 3 years I have found a part of me that had been drugged and tied up in the basement for

decades. I let her out into the daylight and she has been growing stronger each day.

I can barely believe the things I have accomplished since that day from hell 3 years ago. I am in awe of the person I have become and even more in awe of the person I know I will be at the end of 2020.

Every day I remind myself who I am and who I am becoming with this statement:

My name is Kelly Kaye Walker and I am a force of nature. I am divine, determined, and diligent; a valiant daughter of God and a queen in the making. I am a warrior of light and I shine brighter every day, lighting the world more powerfully and irresistibly everywhere I go. As my influence spreads across the nation and the world, I find, inspire and encourage other world-changers to also stand up, be seen, and live their purpose at a higher level. Together we are creating a huge ripple effect of love, light and hope that spreads to every corner of this world.

So I ask you, my fellow world-changer, who are you?

What hell are you going through to become the future version of yourself that makes you cry in gratitude when you catch a glimpse of how YOU will change the world?

Don't let shame and discouragement overcome your transformation. Ask what you need to learn or become from your current challenges, burdens, and even tragedies.

Please believe that this is all for your greater good. You will reach the hearts of those you are here to serve because of what you are learning from this trial.

I see you. Keep going. We need your light. We have a world to change together.

→ Now You Try It! ←

Make a list of things you want to have, be, be or do in the next 6 months. Don't edit yourself with 'realistic' expectations. Through limitations out the window and let your imagination run with the idea. This is similar to a bucket list, only much sooner than "before you kick the bucket." Write it all out and read it every day for 3 weeks with feelings of excitement and gratitude that these things are coming for you now. And any time you hear the 'you can't do that' voice, call it a liar and dismiss it.

SHE BELIEVED SHE
COULD,
AND SO SHE DID.
—
R.S. GREY

Chapter 3

How I Learned to Manifest
(15 Years After Reading The Secret)

I learned the concept of manifesting at a three day seminar that changed my life. A few months later, I attended an Ideal Life Vision retreat where I learned how to write and record the story of my ideal life and listen to it every day. I started out small by claiming that I woke up naturally by 4:30 am or earlier every day, refreshed and ready to go. Previously I had needed about 10 hours of sleep every night and slept as late as possible every morning.

Within a couple weeks, I was waking up at 3:30 am every day and wishing I had left out the phrase "or earlier." (lesson learned!) But instead of going back to sleep, I would get up and go to the living room to do my new morning routine. I had given myself about 4 more hours a day to get things done, which I really needed with all of my new goals and daily habits!

I also listened to myself say "my body is 100% healthy and whole, and my immune system works perfectly" every day. I used to get very sick every fall and several times during the winter for my entire life up to then. Now I am almost never sick and if I am, it is much shorter in duration. I am forever grateful to Laurie Larsen who ran that amazing retreat, gave me that powerful health affirmation, and helped me experience my first success at manifesting.

Soon I went from thinking the Law of Attraction was completely beyond my grasp, to seeing the power of manifesting as doable and repeatable. I wanted to share it with everyone! I started to make it my focus as a speaker and then as a coach.

After a couple of years spent experimenting and tweaking, I found the version that works the best for me. Thus, my 6 Step Formula was born. It may not be the exact recipe that will work for you. But it will definitely start you firmly on the path to mastering the art of manifesting for yourself.

I believe that any person can use the formula to achieve any goal, as long as it is aligned with the laws of the universe. No sprouting wings from your back, or spontaneous teleporting (oh, how I wish I could teleport!), but anything that follows the laws of physics can be achieved.

Here is a short list of some of the things I have manifested in the last couple of years:

Year long speaking/mentoring training course
Winning a speaking contest
Becoming a speaker
Increasing my monthly income x30
Meeting some of my heroes
Speaking in London

Hosting 2 themed cruises
Hair extensions (not everything has to be epic!)
Private coaching session with my coaching/speaking idol
A podcast
16K downloads of my podcast
Amazing coaching clients who are going to change the world with me
A trip to Paris
Going to the top of the Eiffel Tower in Paris
Eating quiche and croissants in Paris
A visit to the Louvre in Paris
Did I mention Paris? (I might be the most excited about that one.)

Shortly before I developed my manifesting formula, I tried achieving my goals by only using a vision board. For those of you unfamiliar with vision boards, they are a poster or cork board with pictures of what you want on them. I had read about a man who was making a vision board and found a picture of a beautiful mansion in a magazine that he cut out and put on his board. Many, many years later he was going through an old box of stuff and found his old vision boards. He was stunned to see the picture of that beautiful mansion he had cut out because it was a picture of his current home!

That story inspired me like nothing before ever had. I believed in the power of vision boards at a cellular level after reading that story! When I made mine, I started out with a small goal, and a picture of it stuck to a white poster board from the dollar store. I added a handwritten description below the picture and, voila, my vision board was born. Each morning I would look at the picture, read the description, then check my thoughts for an idea that might be popping up. If there was no idea, I went on with my day. If there was an idea forming, I would either go do it right then, or make a note to do it when I could.

One of the very first pictures that I put on my vision board was a split end trimmer. It's a cool gadget that opens and closes a bit like a curling iron but has a little motor that turns two spinning blades in a clear plastic housing. You clamp it over a small section of hair and then slide it down all the way past the ends of your hair. I had tons of split ends and wanted one of those gadgets very badly. They were $100, which I didn't have at the time. So I decided to try manifesting a split end trimmer. I put it on my vision board and I was constantly looking at them on online. I was longing and yearning and imagining using one to make my hair sleek and beautiful!

And then I got a crazy idea. What if I found the contact info of the company and proposed a deal? What if I asked them to send me one FOR FREE and if I loved it (which I was sure I would), I would not only write a review, I would do a VIDEO review!? I would also do a blog post about it! I would put it on my YouTube channel!

It seemed highly improbable that anyone would accept my offer because at the time I thought of this, I had a much smaller social media following than I do know.

But the idea had come to me, so I decided to act as if it were an inspired next step and just do it. I figured out how to contact the company. I sent my carefully crafted email and waited.

A response came the next day! I was so excited to read it! But I was also a little scared that they were going to chew me out for making such a ridiculous request. I read the email and was very happily surprised. They made me a counter offer of a very steep discount and a promise from me to send the link to my video review as soon as it was done.

I immediately responded with a "yes" and they responded with instructions. I paid my much-less-than-$100 price and couldn't wait for delivery.

About a week later, my package came. I opened it up and plugged it in to charge and got my hair ready to trim. I used that split end trimmer many times, sent my video review to Amazon, sent the link to the seller, and enjoyed the fruits of my vision board labor.

It was so exciting that I had actually manifested something and that I had obviously been inspired to take very specific action steps, like emailing that company, to make it happen.

It was a completely foreign experience to me. How could putting up a picture of something you want, and then looking at it every day, make any difference? It seemed crazy to me at first, but when I had that split end trimmer in my hands, I knew there was something to it that I just didn't understand yet - something that could make my manifesting work even faster. It was the beginning of the formula I would later discover. I had just unknowingly experienced steps 2, 5, and 6: visualization, inspiration, and implementation.

Facebook Post:

Manifesting My Moby Dick of a Stage

I had a passionate goal the entire first year of my training – to speak on my favorite mentor's stage. Kris Krohn held powerful, life-changing three day events every month and one day I was going to speak on his stage.

Last fall he re-branded. He told me he wasn't doing those events anymore and he would be the only one on stage now, instead of the 10 or so other speakers.

I cried for a week. I was devastated. My year-long goal was completely unattainable. I let it fade and the disappointment slowly faded away too.

He built a new event center in Provo and now has his new multi-day events there, but not monthly, and the new event is very different.

And then something very unexpected happened to me 2 weeks ago. I had been invited to speak at an event on January 25, 2020 by my friend Diana Groesbeck at her Ladies in Action networking meeting. Of course I said yes because I love her and I love speaking. I didn't even ask where the event was going to be, and it didn't matter – I would go anywhere in Utah happily.

Two weeks ago, I finally happened to read the location of the event and my jaw dropped. I got super emotional and had an unexpected flood of tears.

The location is Kris Krohn's new event center.

I am speaking on Kris's stage.

He won't be there, and it's not his event, but I am speaking on his stage.

The emotions are swirling and I'm not sure what they all are, but there is wonder at my power of manifesting, excitement at fulfilling an old impossible goal, amusement that I wasn't more specific in my *manifesting, gratitude to finally speak on his stage, fear that I won't live up to my vision of someone powerful enough to be on that particular stage, and worried I won't be able to fully take advantage of all the amazing AV effects that stage is capable of.*

So here's my chance to conquer my Moby Dick of stages. The one that got away, the one that is miraculously back in my reach. I will be speaking on The Drive-Thru Method of Manifesting... on a stage I believed I could never manifest.

→ Now You Try It! ←

Choose something small and attainable to manifest - like something you could go buy at the store. Get a picture of it and look at it very attentively. Notice every detail about it. Then listen for any ideas to pop up into your mind. Do the idea immediately if you can. If not, make a note to do it asap. Repeat every day until the item comes into your possession.

> Most people are thinking about what they don't want, and they're wondering why it shows up over and over again.
>
> — John Assaraf

Chapter 4

What You Focus on Grows
(The Reticular Activating System)

I want you to try a little guided imagery with me.

Imagine that you are at a red carpet event. You're with a group of very successful-looking people and all of you are dressed in elegant gowns and tuxedos. You are walking down the red carpet towards the entrance to the fanciest event you have ever attended in your life.

Just as you reach the doorway, there is a red velvet rope blocking your way. Standing in front of you is a big, burly bouncer with an earpiece in his ear and a clipboard in his hand. He scans you sternly, asking for your name. When you tell him, he looks down at the clipboard for a long moment. The moment draws out from long to awkward as you see him make it to the bottom and start over again at the top. He's scanning the VIP List for your name before he lets you in. What happens if your name isn't on it? You aren't getting in.

Ok, come back to reality.

Did you get a solid image of the bouncer? Can you picture him clearly? I will tell you what mine looked like if you want to borrow this image for your bouncer. He's about 6'4" with short dark hair, nice stubble, piercing blue eyes, bulging muscles, dressed all in black and he doesn't smile much. He's kind of a cross between Dwayne Johnson and Tony Robbins. Can you see him? Awesome! Now that you have that image in your head, I want you to know something really important.

YOU ACTUALLY HAVE A BOUNCER IN YOUR HEAD!

Look at your pinky finger. There is a bundle of nerves at the base of your brain, just above your spinal column that is the size of your pinky finger called the Reticular Activating System, or RAS for short. Tiny but mighty, it acts as the bouncer to the door to your brain. Though it is small in size, it is huge in power!

The purpose of this powerful little bouncer is to filter out any sensory input that it thinks you don't need to worry about or waste time on. Every second, your mind is bombarded with billions of bits of information. If you had to attend to every one of these, it would completely overload your mind and, I suspect, instantly turn you into a vegetable.

Your RAS is the big burly bouncer at the door to the VIP event that is your brain! It looks at all the billions of bits of information, checks which ones are on your VIP List, then only lets in those most important, desirable bits - and sends all the rest packing.

Where do you suppose your bouncer gets that VIP List? He gets it from you! You are creating that list with your reactions, behaviors, and language every day.

Anything you think about, cry about, worry about, get excited about, love, fear, or dread goes on your list. These are things that your bouncer knows are important to you because they are always on your mind.

If you can only see around 100 of the billions of bits of information around you at any second, what happens to the things NOT on your list?

They are 100% invisible to you.

Which means that if something isn't on your VIP list, even if it's the answer to your life-long question, the solution to your biggest most destructive problem, the key to making a million dollars this year, YOU CAN'T SEE IT!

The perfect client ready to buy your biggest program, the new supplement that could restore your health, are all around you - right in your line of sight even, but if you focus on being broke, not being able to get clients, and all your physical ailments, your bouncer won't let them past the red velvet rope and into your brain, so you never even know they exist.

I have good news for you though. It is actually very easy to rewrite your VIP List if you know how. In fact, there's a good chance you have rewritten your VIP List in a very significant way already if you have ever bought a car.

Go back to the year before you bought your car. How often did you notice that car, in your color, a year before you bought it? Not very often, right? Now fast forward to the year after you bought that car. I can almost guarantee that you saw that car way more frequently!

So what happened? Did your whole town go out and buy the same car as you did that day? No. Your new car went onto your VIP List. All the times you passed that car before you bought it, your bouncer filed it in the Not Important pile, so it was invisible to you. Those cars were all around you, but you didn't notice them because that car wasn't important enough to make the cut. By purchasing that car, you sent it from 'invisible' to VIP list status overnight!

Remember, what you focus on grows, so what you focus on goes onto your VIP List and you start noticing more and more of it. Do the actual numbers of the item change, or does your perception change? That saying that your thoughts create your reality is scientific fact. And your bouncer with your VIP List is how that science takes place in your brain.

A few years ago I was suffering from a pretty deep depression, I had just been fired, and I had no idea what to do with my life. And then, I was invited to a 3-day personal development seminar. Suddenly I became aware of motivational speakers, coaching, experiential processes, and my VIP list went crazy with new entries! I was obsessed and I wanted more!

That world that had previously been completely unknown to me suddenly became my whole world. The emotions I felt at those events were so strong that my VIP list was almost completely rewritten within about 3 months.

Depression faded to the background and soon disappeared completely. I developed a burning desire to be on stage, changing lives, and becoming a huge influencer for good. My RAS started seeing opportunities for growth in that direction everywhere I looked.

I remember thinking how weird it was that there had been this entire culture of personal development right under my nose and I had never caught even a glimpse of it. Within a year, I had my first 2 coaching clients and I was speaking on stages around the valley.

My RAS was on fire for chances to speak and it led me to more and more stages until I ended up in London, England speaking to a room full of international business women on manifesting clients for their business. I couldn't have even IMAGINED myself speaking to ANY audience in London 3 years ago. When you change your RAS, you literally change your reality!

Experiencing strong emotions over something is a highly effective way to ensure something gets added to your VIP list. While emotions are excellent 'anchors' for our VIP list, they aren't the only way to add something to the list. Another way is repetition.

Saying something over and over again for weeks or months or even years, whether in your head or out loud, puts it on your VIP list. I bet you know someone that always says "I can't afford it." No matter what happens, they will never be able to afford it. They have repeated it so often for so long that their RAS only lets them see things to support their belief that they can't afford anything

Some call that self-fulling prophecy. I call it manifesting on accident.

There are ways to make money all around that person every day, but because they regularly repeat the mantra "I can't afford it" their RAS has to ignore those obvious ways to make money. Their RAS thinks that they are more safe and more comfortable if they don't have money to spend on anything.

Luckily for us, because the RAS adds new things to the VIP list based on emotions and repetition, we can pretty easily use emotions and repetition to our advantage when trying to manifest something new. In order to change what you notice, and therefore change what you have, you have to change some items on your VIP list.

Do you think that you might have a thing or two on your list that need to be removed ASAP? I sure did! You can use the following strategies to change your VIP list.

First, start repeating several times a day the thing you want, as if it were already yours. If you want to stop manifesting money problems, and start manifesting a larger income, say out loud several times a day that you are so blessed to have money flowing so easily and abundantly into your life, your hands, and your bank accounts. Talk about how amazing your relationship with money is now, and how awesome it was to heal your money flow! Speak out loud the story of your perfect money situation multiple times a day!

Second, to make the repetition work even better, get emotional about it! Bring up the feelings of gratitude and relief you are going to feel when you actually are experiencing a greater cash flow, all your bills are paid with money left over, and you feel a new sense of freedom you have never felt before!

Think about the people you will be able to help, the places you'll be able to visit, the problems you'll be able to solve for your loved ones, and the ripple effects that will happen because you are so blessed financially! Tap into your emotions - they are powerful!

A great way to sum up the whole Reticular Activating System process is this: **what you focus on grows.**

Whatever you focus on, whether positive or negative, you will see more of in your life. One of the main things I work with clients on is changing their focus from what they don't want and shifting it onto what they do want.

Unfortunately, it's a lot easier to focus on what you don't want because those things usually cause strong negative emotions.

I have learned this lesson the hard way over and over again as I have focused on the things I didn't want, and the things in my life that upset me.

Remember the example in the beginning of this book where I was trying to heal my vision by focusing on how much I hated wearing glasses! I see so many people trying to make changes in their lives by focusing on hating the current state of something.

Money, weight, and clutter are the biggest challenges I have seen people face. It's hard to force your mind to focus on prosperity when you are overdrawn and the power is about to be shut off, but it can be done!

When trying to release weight, it's so tempting to look at your rolls with disgust and shame - but that only reinforces the image of your body in an overweight state!

And when you look around your house and see the clutter, your natural reaction is usually overwhelm and hopelessness

- so your RAS feels that emotion and makes sure you keep experiencing clutter.

Training your mind to ignore the reality of your current situation and picture your goal with excitement and gratitude feels like an impossible task, but it's not. I know it's possible because I have done it and I have changed my reality so drastically in the last 3 years.

My Drive-Thru Method of Manifesting will help you manage what you focus on. It will help you shift your focus from what you don't want to what you DO want! This shift in focus is huge and is the foundation for creating the life of your dreams through manifesting better things. It will help you create a whole new VIP list for your RAS to work with. Every day that you follow the formula, you are working to keep your focus on what you want to manifest, instead of the things you want to stop manifesting.

→ Now You Try It! ←

Try this experiment with a roommate, coworker, or family member who is in the same room with you.

Before you announce the experiment, and without being noticed, sneakily place a couple of small items of the same color in the room, maybe blue for example. Now choose a different color that you can find in several places in the room, such as brown - a lamp, the carpet, the ceiling fan, a picture frame.

To start the experiment, ask the other person to look around the room for 5 seconds and memorize the location of as many brown things as possible and then close their eyes. While their eyes are closed, say "Keeping your eyes closed, lift both arms and point at two different BLUE items."

They will be stupefied and you'll both have a laugh, but think about the ramifications of this 'blindness' they had to blue items. Whatever you focus on grows, and they were only focusing on brown. They didn't notice blue because it wasn't on their VIP list.

Think about how you might be focusing on a negative circumstance in your life, but totally blind to some really great positive things right there in front of you.

EVERYONE HAS A PURPOSE IN LIFE...A UNIQUE GIFT OR SPECIAL TALENT TO GIVE TO OTHERS.

—

DEEPAK CHOPRA

Chapter 5

Manifesting in Alignment With Your Purpose

We are all raised with expectations. Our families and partners love us and want us to be happy, and sometimes their ideas of how we can be the happiest are not in alignment with who we truly are. That doesn't make them bad or controlling, and that doesn't make us rebellious or ungrateful.

It means we all need to learn how to let our loved ones explore and experience consequences as they find their purpose and passion in life, while still loving and accepting them no matter what that purpose and passion turns out to be. It means we all get to understand and love each other as we work on letting go of our ideas of how they would be most fulfilled. It requires love, patience and communication from all parties in order to let go of decades-long expectations that are holding many people back from finding their purpose.

So many people try to squeeze themselves into an image of who they think they should be, and then cut off all circulation to the person they truly are. What happens in nature when you cut off circulation? Things die. What happens when you cut off circulation to your true self? Hopes and dreams die. Sense of identity dies. True purpose dies. Stop starving your true self.

Take that girl out of the basement, untie her, and let her see the light of day! Give her love and attention and validation! Stop trying to be the perfect version of something you aren't.

What has this got to do with manifesting?

Manifesting something that goes against your true self is hard, painful, and a huge waste of your time and energy. Your heart will never be truly in it, and you will experience huge resistance. It will wear you out and turn you against setting goals at all. So to be the best at manifesting you can be, first you need to know your true self.

Why are you here? What is your purpose? Who are you here to serve? How are you meant to change the world? These questions matter. They probably scare the living daylights out of you sometimes. The closer you get to the truth, the scarier they can be.

One of our biggest fears is that we are glorious, powerful beings that have a light so bright it can't help but light up everything around us. Success is so much scarier than failure. Influencing the world is so much scarier than hiding in the background. But that's not what you were born for.

Hiding is not your mission. Embracing your true self, living your purpose, and impacting the world for good is your mission! It's a mission all of us were born with, but so many have lost track of, or lost themselves, or just shut down after one too many failures.

It's time to put on your big girl panties and decide that you are ready to face your fears. Decide right now that you are brave enough to learn about your own gigantic potential and start embracing your true self. You don't have to be that perfect Pinterest mom! You don't have to be that effortless Instagram influencer! You don't have to be some watered-down or beefed-up version of a woman that seems like she's got it all together. (BTW, she doesn't!) Figure out who YOU are, and what it is you want to do with that. Find your core and discover your purpose. Stop trying to be someone you're not, because you're ripping us all off by not being YOU.

How do you find your purpose?

I have an awesome purpose-finding workshop that I am adapting here for you to do on your own. All you need to do is follow the instructions, being completely honest with yourself. Nobody will see your answers but you, so be 100% honest. If you're fake, you'll get fake results.

Before you start this exercise, grab a notebook and pen and go to a quiet, comfortable spot. Once you get yourself settled in, start with getting grounded. That means to close your eyes and focus only on your breathing. Try to make each breath slower and deeper than the last one. After 5 or 6 breaths, imagine a bright white light shining down on you. It passes into your body, traveling from the top of your head to the bottoms of your feet, lighting up every cell of your body on the way. As it passes through you, it burns out all doubt, confusion, and distraction - leaving only peace and love. This beam of light goes all the way into the ground, through the layers of the earth, connecting you from your higher power above to Mother Earth below. You are now grounded and can begin the exercise.

→ Now You Try It! ←

Are you ready to dive into finding your purpose? Schedule some 'me' time where you can sit, uninterrupted, get grounded, and really get honest and open with yourself. When you are ready, answer the following questions:

1. Examine your abilities objectively: what are your greatest strengths? This isn't bragging, just observing.

2. What activities do you love so much that you could actually forget to stop and eat or want to stay up all night doing them?

3. What is a common thread? (i.e. are they all about creating something, or building connections with people, or solving a problem, etc.)

4. What are your biggest regrets? What decisions do you wish you had made?

5. What are your top 5 happiest memories? Where were you, who were you with, what were you doing?

6. Name five qualities of someone you admire a lot. Now see that you have those same qualities or you wouldn't have been drawn to them.

7. What would you spend your time doing if money were no issue and you could make a billion dollars morally, legally, and ethically at any moment, forever?

8. What positive things do people say about you most often?

9. What has been your dream job, ignoring all obstacles real or imagined?

10. What is the biggest trial you have dealt with?

11. How did you overcome that trial? What steps did you go through? How can you help others going through the same trial?

12. Ask your future self what made the biggest difference in your life. Also ask your future self what was the least important thing you spent time on?

Look over your answers. Re-ground yourself if needed and ask for your intuition to guide you to the truth of who you are and why you are here. Sometimes our 'common sense' can be too judgmental and bat away the truth when it comes up. Give yourself permission to see and hear all inspiration no matter how unlikely it may seem.

As you contemplate your inspired thoughts, you will start to see the bigger picture of your purpose and why you are here. Journal everything that comes up. Write down what you think your purpose might be. Don't worry about it being right, or about it having to be forever. Just let whatever comes to you go down on paper. Write it all out.

In a day or two, go back and read what you wrote. Let new thoughts come up and write them down too. Zoom in a bit on what your purpose might be. Take another day or two to let it digest, then revisit it. The process could take days, weeks or even months. Be patient and be honest. It will come to you.

So how do you know if you have found your purpose and are living it? If your day is filled with contentment, positivity and gratitude then you are much closer to living your purpose than if your days were full of stress, complaining, regrets and lethargy.

Living your purpose will energize you and fill you with peace, happiness and a sense of accomplishment. Your mind will expand and be open to new ideas that contribute to your purpose. You will feel yourself progressing and it will be amazingly powerful.

Living your purpose will feel totally different than drifting through life aimlessly. Doors will open for you, things will always fall into place, and miracles will become a frequent occurrence for you.

Blog Post

When I was young, I had a very strong need to keep my family members calm and safe. As the oldest of 4, I was often shifting into the mother role as early as I can remember. Watching my younger sisters playing with Barbies, I remember only wanting to play with baby dolls and easy bake ovens when I was their age. I wondered what was wrong with me because Barbies held no attraction for me. I wanted to take care of babies and bake while they wanted to have glamorous fashion adventures. My mothering instinct was strong.

As we got older and were first children of very unhappily married parents, and then became children of divorced parents, we all experienced much drama, trauma, and instability. I formed deep subconscious beliefs that I had to make sure everyone was ok before I could even think about being ok myself. In fact, the process of keeping everyone else ok is what I began to interpret as me being ok. Once in family therapy the therapist said I was a peacemaker, and that it wasn't a good thing. I was setting aside my own progress and happiness to worry about the safety and sanity of my family.

Today I was having a session with the amazing Angela Smart, clearing out old trapped emotions. The process was deep and emotional and epic. Something that came up was a reluctance to reach my potential because it might hurt my family. Not my husband and son, but my parents and siblings. I discovered that I had been living by the self-imposed rule that I can't go be awesome until all my siblings are ok. Or until my mom is ok.

Now, ok is a relative term and everyone has their own definition and measuring stick of their level of 'ok-ness.' I know my parents and siblings have hurts and challenges just like everyone else does. And I know they are all progressing and learning and growing at their perfect pace. So I can let go of that silly, hindering gate I placed in front of me, holding off on going through it until everyone else is done with their trials and challenges and goes through the gate first. Maybe, I realized today, they NEED me to go through that gate first. Maybe my brave steps through that gate and beyond are something they *all desperately crave on a subconscious level. Maybe my waiting for them to all be ok is actually keeping them from being ok.*

Or maybe not. It could be that I just need to break free of my self-imposed limits and doubts for me, and it has nothing to do with them. Either way, my next steps are clear. Go through the gate. Don't worry about where other people are on their path to the gate. Stop making up worst case scenarios of what will happen to them when I shake off the chains and fly through that gate. Just go through the gate already. Whatever happens, it will definitely be better than holding back and shying away from reaching my potential.

It couldn't possibly be worse than that.

THE REASON MOST PEOPLE NEVER REACH THEIR GOALS IS THAT THEY DON'T DEFINE THEM.

—

DENIS WAITLEY

Chapter 6

Step # 1: Clarification

You are hungry and driving down a road where both sides are filled with fast food places. Some are highly enticing, some you don't give a second thought. So many of them are vying for your attention, for your business, for your taste buds. BOGOs and discounts and sales, oh my! How on earth do you decide where you want to eat with so many great choices?

This is where you decide which drive-through sounds the most appealing to you right now. Are you hungry for a burger and fries with a chocolate shake? Do you need to crunch on some tacos? Are chicken sandwiches and frozen lemonade calling to you? Or maybe a gigantic breakfast burrito from the all-night Mexican place? No wait - a salad!

There are countless options, but in order to eat (get your goal) you have to start by CHOOSING one of the countless options! Getting really clear on what they want is usually the hardest step for most of my clients. (The second hardest is usually Step #6 - spoiler alert!)

If you're going to get something different than you have now (like a full belly instead of hunger), you have to get clear on what you want. Want a new love interest? Not getting clear on what you want usually leads to attracting the same person in a different body over and over again. To avoid that mistake, I have my clients make a full profile of the person they want to have in their life, from what side of the bed they prefer to how they like their steak cooked. Write it all out.

Want a new job? The same principle applies. Decide exactly what a day at your new job is like from the time you get there to the time you leave. What city do you want to work in? How much do you want to be paid? How do you want to feel at the end of the day? Write it all out.

Need money? Get specific! How much do you want? When do you want it? What do you want it for? How will you spend it? How soon will you spend it? What account would you like to show up in? Write it all out.

You can apply this to literally anything you want to manifest. When you create a fully detailed vision of what you want in your head and then write it all down, you will have the level of clarity needed to successfully manifest it!

I can hear some of you thinking right now, "But what if I don't know what I want?"

If you find that you don't really know what you want, you are not alone. I have found that most people don't. They are too caught up in daily life to give their wants any thought at all. Just taking care of all their responsibilities each day uses up all of their energy, leaving none for thinking about the future or their desires. In fact, one thing everyone seems to have no trouble with at all is knowing what they DON'T want. Often when I ask a new client what they want, they immediately answer, "Well, I don't want …." When I gently point out their failure to answer my actual question, they get perplexed or frustrated and sometimes even emotional because they have no idea what they really want.

I want to point out here that this is not a failure. It's important to know that learning what you don't want is always a step in the right direction towards figuring out what you do want. One of the things we learn from unpleasant experiences is that we definitely don't want certain things. Learning the contrast is valuable. But no matter how long your list of 'don't wants' is, actually coming up with a list of things you specifically DO want is sometimes a daunting task.

Most people can name a few things they would enjoy, but in general there is a lack of dreaming big. What do you really want? What will bring you the most satisfaction, fulfillment and happiness? Do you have a bucket list? If you aren't choosing now the amazing experiences you want to have in the future, your mind has no way to get you there. You could end up living your life with no goals set and no goals met and that can lead to no intense joy felt, no deep sense of purpose fulfilled. Living a surface-level life sounds very sad and empty, and I hope to influence everyone I can to live a more meaningful version of their life.

If you were brought up being taught that it's selfish to want different things than you currently have, then you have probably spent years trying to shut down your ability to come up with new desires and dreams. But there is no shame in knowing and going after what you want. We were not born to wander aimlessly and have no desires. I believe we were sent here to learn how to love ourselves and each other, how to live in and control a body of flesh and blood, and experience contrast to learn exactly what we want so that we can reach consistently higher levels of happiness.

Troubleshooting the Clarity Step

The "And vs. Or" Conundrum

With most of my clients, I have seen that their main struggle with getting clear is that they are scared that once they make a decision, they are somehow permanently rejecting a lot of the other things they want. I am not a fan of that false and limiting philosophy. I happily subscribe to the "AND not OR" way of thinking.

We aren't ruling out other possibilities when we make a choice. We are simply saying "This is what I want now, AND I am saving these other desires for later." Later might be later today, later this week, or later this year.

You may be one of those people who feel like choosing one manifestation to focus on means that someone has dropped a giant "OR" into your life. Money for a trip OR money for a new car. Start a new business OR write a book. Learn a new language OR plan and build a tiny home. Choosing one feels like giving up on the other. You have a multitasking brain for a reason! You can manifest more than one thing at a time - or immediately after achieving the previous thing. You can have anything you want, in any order you want, or even simultaneously.

The "Life or Death" Conundrum

In the case of the Drive-Thru analogy, consider the short-term commitment you are making to your goal. One meal. That's it. Maybe 20 minutes of your life. One dinner choice is not earth-shattering. It is not a life or death situation. And if you get home and there are pickles when you specifically asked for no pickles, it does not result in instant death by starvation. After an eye roll and exasperated sigh, you simply remove the pickles and eat your food anyway.

If people could channel some of the casual attitude of dinner decisions into their beginning attempts with manifesting, I think most of them would have a much easier time with step #1. In fact, when starting to experiment with your own manifesting adventures, I suggest starting with something very small and trivial but fun to have - something that won't crush you if it comes late, or in a different color, or any other way that could be disappointing because you didn't expect it. Something like a split end trimmer. That worked so well as a first manifestation because it wasn't something I desperately needed, but it was really fun to have once I got it.

The "I Must Be Crazy" Conundrum

Do you ever feel like that thing you want is crazy? Or that you are weird to want the thing you want? Or that it's too big? Have you ever wondered what other people want to manifest in their lives? Well, you don't have to wonder anymore. I am going to give you a peek into the minds of people who were willing to share the things they want most. You will see that you are in good company with people who are dreaming big, small, and everywhere in between!

Job that I love
Own our house
Ability to help others
Write/Finish/Publish a book
Abundance/Money/Financial freedom
Travel
A baby
Peace
More Clients
Better health
Less weight
Host amazing retreats
Sell my home
Find my niche
Confidence

Success in my business
Healthier, happier relationships
The love of my life
A spouse
De-clutter my house
Clarity on what I want
Energy and passion
Speaking gigs
More me time
Spiritual guidance
A fresh start
Online course
Happiness
A sauna
A trip to Hogwarts (at Universal Studios)
Early retirement
Miracles
Unshakable faith
Teach a class at a Tony Robbins conference
A 1000 sq ft apartment
Getting my drivers license back
A farm
Trip to Bermuda
Get rid of a certain love interest
Disneyland trip
Becoming a speaker
Calmness

Kelly Kaye Walker

And, in case you were wondering, here are some of the things I want to manifest in the next year:

Finish my book and become a New York Times Bestseller
Hold at least 4 full-day sold out Manifesting events
Move into a new house
Hire an assistant and a housekeeper
1 million downloads of my podcast
A white Mazda CX-5 with the Grand Touring package and custom trim

→ Now You Try It! ←

Baby step your way to clarity on what you want! Start a list that you add to every time you get an urge to have, do, or be something. Always go write it down before you forget. Or create the list on your phone if that is more convenient. Over time you will have a nice list of things you might want to manifest. Writing it down doesn't set it in stone - this list will just be a receptacle for your ideas that you can choose whether to act on or discard later.

WE BECOME WHAT WE THINK ABOUT MOST OF THE TIME.

—

EARL NIGHTINGALE

Chapter 7

Step #2: Visualization

You've decided where to go for dinner. You are pulling up to the brightly lit menu board. Enticing pictures of food start you salivating and suddenly you feel your stomach growl. Food! So many choices! So many up-sells! So many combinations! Look at those photos, focus on the details, imagine taking a bite and how it's going to taste.

Those onion rings look like heaven on earth - better get those. Feel the crunch of the batter and then the squish of the onion. Maybe get a large instead of a medium. Fry sauce and ketchup because AND not OR. See the burger you want and picture it with mayo dripping out the back when you bite it. Oh no - a pickle! Note to self - remember to ask for no pickles. Look at the glistening photos of the sodas on ice with sparkling condensation forming on the outside. Visualize taking a sip of that one - oh wait, remember no ice so it doesn't get watered down.

This step calls for you to see, in excruciating detail, the thing you want. You need to see every aspect of it, every nuance, every effect it will have on your life, how others will react to it, how you will be different with it, and more.

The reason that visualization is so important is that you're teaching your brain what you want by experiencing it as if you've already done it. Your brain is hardwired to keep you where you currently are, because change is scary! Change might cause discomfort, which could lead to death! It seems irrational to our conscious brain, but there is a part of our subconscious brain that is very scared that we might go off the rails and get ourselves involved in something dangerous that could lead to, yep, you guessed it, death.

Our brains have a very clear picture of what is acceptable and what is dangerous. It doesn't like for us to even look at things that are dangerous, and it especially doesn't like us to think about them, and visualizing them is absolutely out of the question!

Luckily for us, our brains are created to be lazy. In other words, our brains prioritize saving energy over other functions. So, if you keep visualizing the thing you want, your brain will eventually get tired of using all that extra energy to fight your vision.

Like the persistent toddler that asks and begs and pleads his mother for something long enough that she finally gives in, our brains eventually give in to the visualization of the new thing we want. That point comes when your brain calculates that it will be easier to stop spending energy on that battle and it's more energy efficient to give up and stop fighting us. Everyone's point is different, because everyone's brain is different. There is no way to know your brain's retreat point so just keep visualizing and manifesting until it happens.

Visualizing For Your Learning Type

There are 3 main types of learners: Visual, Auditory, and Kinesthetic/Tactile.

Visual learners receive the most information through their eyes. They even tend to have larger eyes proportionately than other types of learners. Visualizing through images is the easiest for this type of learner. They naturally picture the things they want and have the most success at filling in the visual details of their creation. A vision board is one of the best ways for visual learners to manifest what they want on a daily basis.

Auditory learners learn best through hearing. These are your audiobook lovers, musicians, and language buffs. They love listening to sounds and creating their own. Visualizing is different for the auditory learner. In their "visualizations", they focus on sounds, ambient noise, rhythms, voices, words, and soundtracks. They are more prone to hear their goal come to life than to see their goal in full detail. Creating a recording of what they'd like to manifest is one of the best ways for auditory learners to manifest.

The kinesthetic/tactile learners involve movement and touch when they are learning. They will prefer to visualize how their goal feels, how it will involve motion and movement, how their body will react with the goal and anything else that can be felt or touched. Going and actually touching the item (along with smelling, seeing, and hearing it…please don't taste it) is one of the best ways kinesthetic/tactile learners can help themselves to manifest.

Your "visualizing" should be the right type for your learning style. Don't try to fit into the style of someone else - that is a sure way to get burned out and give up on manifesting. Honor your strengths and use them to your full advantage.

The level to which you need to go in visualizing is probably a lot deeper than you have experienced before. The more detailed you get, the more quickly and easily you will manifest the object of your visualization. I will give some examples to show how much detail you need to add to yours.

How Detailed Do You Need To Get?

New Job: Detail Level - Ninja!

Let's say your goal is a new job. Here are some questions to ask yourself in order to create a fully detailed vision of this new job in your mind so that you can manifest it.

What city do you work in?

How do you feel at the end of day?

The Drive-Thru Method of Manifesting

What kind of environment do you want to work in? Cubicles? At home? Corner office?

How many people are in your office? Or are you home, or maybe traveling?

What's the general energy of the room you work in? Excited? Calm? Playful?

What's the dress code? What do you wear? Do you need to go shopping for clothes?

Is there music playing or will it be silent? Is there lots of happy chatter or quiet concentration?

How is the temperature? Do you have a cozy blanket there? Fan to cool you off? Just right?

Is the lighting natural or artificial? Can you control the lighting?

Can you see outside? Are there windows everywhere or just a few here and there?

Do you take your lunch or eat out? Is there a group you eat with? Cafeteria on site?

What hours do you work? Are they flexible? Can you set your own hours?

How much do you get paid? Do you get perks? Company car? Laptop to take home?

What benefits do you have? Medical? Dental? Free breakfast or lunch each day?

What kind of a commute do you have? Do you drive or take the train? Carpool? Zoom call only?

How creative do you get to be? Or how number-crunching do you get to be?

Where do you spend your breaks? Awesome breakroom with games? Outside? Nap room?

What do you have on your desk? Decorated or minimalist? Messy or organized?

Do you even have a desk? Maybe you have a standing desk. Or you don't work with desks.

What about company parties? Potlucks? Big catered affairs? Huge Christmas bashes?

How does the boss treat you? Like a valued team member? Like an indispensable expert?

What kind of banter will you have with your co-workers? Will you laugh a lot? Play jokes?

Or are you the boss? Are you in charge of a department? Or a whole company?

Slimming Down: Detail level - Skinny Jeans!

What about dropping some weight? Just about everyone I know would love to drop at least 10 pounds, and some would like to drop 10 times that! Let's look at the ideal level of detail needed for successfully manifesting a slimmer body. Here are some questions to help you get really detailed on releasing weight.

How much do you want to weigh? Why?

What will it feel like to weigh that much? How will it feel to get out of bed in the morning?

What will you be able to do that you haven't been able to do at your current size?

What kind of food will you eat? How will you feel about that?

Where will you eat? Kitchen? Candlelit dining room? Car?

How many times a day will you eat? Intermittent fasting? 6 small meals?

How will you decide what to eat? Meal planning or whatever sounds good at the moment?

When will you do food prep? As you cook, once a week, or a month of freezer meals in a day?

What will you take your food in when you have to go to a long meeting? Or will you eat out?

What will you do with your clothes as you shrink out of them? Donate? Take them in? Save?

What emotions will you have as you reveal a slimmer body? Confidence? Pride? Excitement?

How will you deal with the negative emotions that come up? Cry? Journal? Belief breakthrough?

How will you conquer obstacles? Step back, analyze, make a plan? Power through? Wing it?

Where will you buy new smaller clothes? What stores? The mall? Boutiques? Online? Thrift?

- How will your exercise routine look? Gym? Walking outside? Home workouts? Yoga? Weights?
- How much water will you drink? When will you do it during the day? How will you measure?
- What medications will you be able to stop taking? What medical conditions will be healed?
- How many years will you add to your life? How much energy will you have?
- What will your kids think of the new thinner you? How will your triumph affect their confidence?
- How will your self-esteem be affected? How much more confidence will you have?
- Who in your life will you inspire? Whose lives will you touch?
- How many people will you inspire as you transform? Hundreds? Thousands? Your family?
- What new adventure will you try? Para-sailing? Rock climbing? Pickleball? Acro yoga?
- What will you do with your hair? Finally get that cute short hair that only works on thin faces?
- How is it going to feel to zip up those goal jeans? What will you do when it happens?
- What vacation are you going to take to celebrate (and maybe flaunt) your new body?
- What will your neck, arms, and legs feel like? What about your stomach? Your chin? Ankles?

The Drive-Thru Method of Manifesting

New Love Interest: Detail Level - Happily Ever After!

What if your goal is to attract a new romantic partner? How specific can you get without creating an over-the-top fictional character that couldn't possibly exist? I have my clients get pretty dang specific here too! Here are some important questions to help you decide WHO you really want.

How old are they?
What do they value?
How passionate are they?
What doesn't matter to them?
How do they spend their down time?
How much down time do they have?
Where do they want to be in 10 years? 20 years?
How do they like to eat dinner?
Are they a morning person?
What side of the bed do they prefer?
How do they feel about surprises?
Do they have a neat streak or are they a bit disorganized?
Do they open the door for you?
How do they get along with their mother, father, siblings?
What are their pet peeves?
Are they a dog person or a cat person? Or a no pet person?
What kind of TV shows do they watch? Do they watch TV?

Kelly Kaye Walker

What's on their bucket list?

Are they ambitious or comfortable?

How do they deal with conflict?

Do they smoke or drink?

How much is music a part of their life and what kind do they listen to?

Are they an introvert or an extrovert?

Are they people-oriented of task-oriented?

What is their love language?

Do they share your political views?

Do they want kids? Do they have kids already?

Do they eat breakfast?

Do they work out?

Are they growth-driven or comfort-driven?

What is their most common mood?

What's their biggest struggle?

What is their biggest strength?

City or country?

DIY or hire a professional?

Early bird or night owl?

And most importantly, how do you feel around them and how do they make you feel about yourself?

The Drive-Thru Method of Manifesting

It may seem daunting to come up with such a detailed idea of something or someone but remember that the quality of your vision determines the speed of your manifesting. Also, be aware that sometimes you are going to manifest something even better than what you imagined. Make sure you are energetically open to that possibility.

If you are too attached to the exact version you are envisioning, you might be blocking something that is even better than you could ever imagine. I like to say 'or something better' when I am figuring out what I want. And if you manifest something that's a 90% match to what you wanted, are you going to be ecstatic or are you going to complain and moan about the 10% difference?

Upgrade Your Visualization Skills with a Vision Board

You have probably heard of a vision board if you have been alive and awake at any point over the last 15 years. They are taking the world by storm and for good reason. A vision board helps you visualize much more clearly because you literally have your goal in front of you in picture form along with a written description! It's like a cheat sheet for your brain, especially when visualization is a challenge for you.

Here are the steps to properly use a vision board

1. Designate a space for your vision board.

I like a framed cork board for several reasons. It's portable. It's easily changed. It's light. I can move pins all I want without damaging the board. And it's easy to find one at the store. You can also use poster board, a specific place on your wall you mark out with painters tape, or even your home screen/wallpaper on your phone/laptop. The most important thing is that it's convenient to get to and you can see it right after waking up and right before going to sleep.

2. Get a picture of the thing you want.

When it's an object, this step is pretty easy. Just go on the internet and find a picture and print it out. Let's say your goal is a trip to Hawaii. You could find photos of an airplane flying over water, photos of Hawaii, or even pictures of plane tickets.

I love the free stock photo site Pixabay.com for finding photos. When it's something less tangible, you will probably have to get creative. If your goal is finishing your book, you might find a picture of a blank book and Photoshop the title of yours onto it, or make a fake NYT Bestseller list with your book at the top. If you don't have Photoshop skills, you can even draw a picture. Draw your book sitting in the window of a bookstore, or something else that represents your book being published.

3. Write a description.

Type up the details of your goal and print them out, or write them down on paper. Add all the details you can come up with. Aim for a full sheet of paper or more if you are really serious about getting your goal. The more details the better! If you run out of details, add some stories of you using or enjoying the thing you want to manifest.

If you were manifesting a new car, in your description you could talk about how awesome it is to have manifested this car and how your family loves to take it on road trips. It's so great for road trips because the back lays down flat for a super comfy sleeping area, and the windows are tinted so it's really private and cozy. You all love the USB charging ports at every seat, and the separate heater and air conditioner controls for each row. The back-up camera is so much safer and the heated seats are amazing in the long cold winters! Tell all the amazing things you and your family love about it!

4. Place the photo and description in the center of your board.

When starting out, you will only have one item. Go ahead and place it right smack in the middle of your vision board. You want it front and center and no weird spacing to distract you. Depending on the shape of your photo, you can put the description next to it or under it. I love thumbtacks on cork board because it's so easy to reposition if I get something crooked or off center at first.

5. Interact with it daily as if you've already achieved it.

Look at it every morning when you first get up and read the description. Feel the gratitude welling up in your heart. Imagine yourself doing or having the thing, with all the happy emotions that come with that experience. If you can convince your subconscious mind that you've already got it and are currently interacting with it on a daily basis, you have won the battle with reality!

Your subconscious knows exactly how to create anything you want in your life, so if it believes you've already done it, it stops trying to hide that knowledge from you and suddenly you have ideas flowing. You just need to believe it for a few minutes each day. It's easier if you have written a full page description of your experience with the item instead of just a short paragraph.

The Drive-Thru Method of Manifesting

The longer you can live in the moment, the sooner you will manifest it. Look at the photo, then read the description, back and forth between the two for at least 3 minutes. Even better - speak out loud all the details of it and how you feel about having it, how your life is affected by it and how your friends and family are affected by it too. Describe all the ripples caused by you achieving this goal.

6. Sit quietly and listen.

Listen for ideas to pop into your mind during or right after your viewing time. Make sure to write them down. When you listen to your thoughts, you may also hear arguments from your brain telling you why you probably can't get that goal. When this happens, you can do a couple different things. First, thank your brain for its input and then inform it that you aren't accepting that information at this time. Acknowledging it is sometimes enough to release it and move on. Second, if it's more insistent and maybe even meaner, write down the negative thoughts to get them out of your brain, then take them outside and burn the paper. This is doubly powerful because not only have you physically removed them from your head, you have reduced them to ashes. It's a great exercise when you find yourself getting discouraged from your negative self talk.

7. Take action.

When an idea comes to you, write it down. And if it's doable right then, go ahead and do it immediately. The sooner the better! If not, schedule it into your calendar to do later that day. Take action on the ideas you receive so you can show your brain you value the ideas it gives you and it can trust you with the next step. If you receive a step and don't do it, you can't expect another step. And some steps are time sensitive so if you don't take action now, a door may close for you.

8. Look at it again right before bed.

As you get in bed and drift off, visualize the details of your vision board item. This gives your subconscious mind something to work on while you are sleeping. Did you know that your subconscious mind gets really bored and does crazy things while you're sleeping if you don't give it an assignment as you fall asleep? Put that supercomputer to work!! Make sure to have a notepad by your bed in case an idea is so exciting it wakes you up in the middle of the night.

9. Keep a record when you reach a vision board goal.

I have a binder full of items I have achieved and taken off my vision board. Get some sheet protectors and each time you get a goal, take the picture and description off the board and put them into a sheet protector and add it to your binder. This binder is proof that you can manifest your goals and that your vision board works. This step is vital to helping you gain confidence and shut down those negative voices that say manifesting is fake and vision boards don't work. You will want to pull out your vision board success binder any time you are feeling like your doubts are getting out of control. Remind yourself that you have manifested before and you can easily do it again!

Your vision board is a living thing. It needs to be updated frequently. If you have a goal that is getting no movement at all, or makes you feel negativity when you look at it, you need to fix it. Your board needs to have positive energy flowing toward it at all times, and a stagnant corner can hinder your manifesting process.

One thing you can do is to journal about the negativity that comes up around that goal. Why does it make you feel that way? Does it bring up an issue you haven't dealt with? Is it too big of a goal and needs to move to a dream board? (Dream boards are for goals that are farther into the future, 2 years or more.)

Another thing you can do is to take it off and break it down into smaller, achievable steps. Then only put one step on your vision board. One step is easier to accomplish.

Also make sure your vision board is in a prime location. If it's tucked away in a cluttered corner, you aren't going to engage with it. Get it out in the open in an easy-to-access spot you can see and interact with easily.

Auditory learners: Record the description of your goal in your own voice. Play epic music in the background that fills you with energy and determination. Listen to this recording during your vision board time. Also read it out loud with music playing. I suggest one session of reading out loud each day and one session of listening to a recording each day.

Kinesthetic/Tactile learners: Go to where you can touch or physically interact with your goal. Record yourself doing so, while pushing every button, opening every door, activating every switch, etc. Video and audio both are best. Every time you watch that video you can see yourself physically interacting with the goal AND hear all the results of your pushing, touching, opening, etc. You will relive the moment every time you watch the video.

→ Now You Try It! ←

Choose your goal to manifest. Write the story of you already having manifested it. Feel the emotions you have, list all the details you can, and express the gratitude you have for that thing already having shown up in your life. Visual? See it from every angle and notice new details you didn't see at first. Auditory? Record the description and listen to it regularly, and also notice any new sounds in your life now that you have achieved your goal. Kinesthetic/Tactile? Act out the story in your mind, imagining the way it feels when you touch it, operate it, enter it, etc. Are there smells? How do you feel around it?

BY WORDS WE LEARN THOUGHTS, AND BY THOUGHTS WE LEARN LIFE.

—

JEAN BAPTISTE GIRARD

Chapter 8

Step #3: Declaration

You're sitting in the drive-thru lane, you've decided exactly what you want to eat, you've visualized it to the point that your mouth is probably watering and your stomach is likely rumbling. The pictures of all the delicious options have thoroughly enticed you, and now it's time to speak your order out loud. You make sure your window is open so your voice can be heard clearly, you lean out a little bit, and you clearly announce what you would like to eat.

This step requires you to open your mouth and tell someone else what you want. You must declare it out loud for it to happen. If you just sat there in silence at the drive-thru - even though you have decided exactly what you want - are you going to receive any delicious, hunger-satisfying food? No! You have to lean out your window towards that microphone hidden somewhere in the drive-thru sign or the bushes and speak your order out loud. If you don't, you will: a. get no food, b. cause a traffic jam, c. upset other people who want to get their food and d. disrupt the flow for everyone around you.

You not speaking your desires out loud hurts you. It prevents you from receiving your desires, it clogs up your manifesting abilities, and it teaches your subconscious that you don't really want what you say you want. What most people don't know is that not speaking your desires out loud can also hurt a lot more people than just yourself! This world was created to be a wish-granting machine and everyone plays a crucial role in that machine - we are all responsible and accountable to different parts of the process at different times.

Everyone has an innate need to give as well as receive. When you hide your desires away, you are stripping those around you of the ability to develop their giving muscles. You are depriving them of blessings they would have otherwise received if they had been allowed to give to you. God yearns to give you what you want, and there are people all around you that have been prepared to help in fulfilling your desires - but you have to ask. If you never ask, the gears in that machine can't even start turning. Say it out loud so someone can give it to you. Put your order out there and get that machine going!

The 3 Protocols: Personal, Positive and Present

Now just speaking your desire out loud is a huge step, and it is so much better than keeping quiet about it. But there are certain ways to express it that are more or less effective than other ways. For the most effective manifesting, I recommend some specific language techniques. Speaking your desires incorrectly can slow down your process, and in some extreme cases, actually reverse the process so you are accidentally repelling your desires.

You may be thinking, "Wait, what? I can speak my goals INcorrectly?!" Yes, you can definitely do this step in a less-effective or even counterproductive way! That's because people just naturally tend to use language in a way that tells the subconscious "Not really - I'm just wishful thinking - I don't really want this goal - please don't let me achieve this!" And even though you will learn how to avoid those pitfalls in this chapter, you will slip and let in a few of the less-effective words and phrases when you repeat your goals out loud every day. That is why I suggest everyone write out their declarations and make sure all the wording is clean and safe for manifesting, instead of just trying to remember to avoid all the pitfalls every single day.

You can accidentally slip in some danger words without realizing it and totally cancel out your manifesting. That's because your subconscious mind is a little bit like a sneaky genie in a bottle. It's always looking for loopholes and other ways to twist what you're saying when you are trying to manifest something it suspects might not be 100% safe and comfortable for you. Remember, it's your subconscious mind's job to keep you alive and comfortable, so anything that takes you out of your comfort zone is totally unacceptable to your subconscious mind. When you have a manifesting script in front of you, with your desires written out in very specific ways, you will always use the best wording to get the most cooperation from your subconscious mind.

These highly important language rules are known as the 3 Protocols. I learned them from my mentor Kris Krohn who is amazing at using language to manifest. Since all three of the Protocols happen to start with the letter P, I usually just call them the 3Ps. They are Personal, Positive, and Present. Because our natural tendency as humans is to violate these protocols in everyday language, it takes mental energy and focus to change the way we speak about our goals.

The first protocol is to keep your declarations Personal.

When you are manifesting something, your language needs to be about how it will change YOU and YOUR behaviors. This is one of those times when it's ok to make it all about you. Your sentences should start with "I" or "My" because you are manifesting something different in YOUR behavior or circumstances. You can add in some mentions of how your goal being achieved will bless someone else, but you can't manifest someone else changing their behavior. Everyone has free will and trying to manifest another human into making a choice you prefer them to make is against the laws of nature. It wastes your energy, it's damaging to your vibration, and it's very bad karma. Now it's ok if your manifesting affects the people around, but never focus on that as the goal. It's only a nice side effect to be appreciated after the fact.

For example: If you want to attract more clients for your business, you may be tempted to phrase it like this: "20 female entrepreneurs see my ad this week and click on my link. They schedule a call with me and 10 of them buy my program before they hang up because they see my expertise and trust me to help them effectively." While that is somewhat effective, the subject is other people over which you have no control. You are directly attempting to manifest a change in their behavior.

The integrous way to phrase it while following the Personal protocol would be: "My ad is being delivered to my ideal clients: female entrepreneurs who desperately need exactly what I provide and are ready and willing to pay to receive it. I am so grateful to get 20 of them on a call, during which I connect with them deeply, use the perfect words that show how completely I understand them, and how effectively I help people like them with their exact issues. My love, confidence and expertise shine through, and now I get to serve 10 new ideal clients next week."

Can you feel the difference between the two declarations? The first one is all about what THEY do. The second one is all about what YOU do. There is much more power in keeping it personal, plus it has a cleaner, kinder energy behind it.

What if you really need someone to change their ways? There is a gentle way to work around the Personal protocol if you are experiencing behavior towards you that needs to stop. But your declaration has to be directed at you and what kind of things you will tolerate and accept. For example: Let's say you have a boss that treats you badly, swears at you, and threatens to replace you with someone more competent and cheaper that you on a regular basis. You may be highly motivated to manifest a change in your boss's behavior and try declaring "My boss sees my value and he appreciates my work." But that's manifesting for him. Here is how you would shift that to follow the Personal protocol: "I am appreciated and valued as an employee. I expect and receive only respect, kindness, and honesty at my workplace."

In the second one, it's all about you and how you experience your work environment. Can that change the behavior of your boss? Actually yes, because you will be putting out a different kind of energy that will subtly inform him that you no longer will accept his bad behavior without you saying a word about it to him. It may be more likely that your new declaration will result in a new job! But you have to be open to that or your fear will block any pathway to a new, better, happier work situation. (I used this example because it is a story from my own life, and it DID result in a new job!)

→ Now You Try It! ←

Take a relationship issue you would like to change and practice writing a declaration that focuses only on you, your feelings, and your behaviors. Make sure you don't mention the other person's behavior at all.

The second protocol is to keep your declaration Positive.

Remember how I tried to manifest better vision by thinking about all the negative effects of wearing glasses? You can not manifest something by focusing on all the things you hate about not having it. Unfortunately, that seems to be the default mode for most people. The pain of something motivates us much more than the promise of pleasure! But focusing on the pain is the surest way to manifest more pain. So first make sure you mention only the thing you want and never the thing you don't want.

Often I hear people say they want to stop smoking, or they want to lose weight, or they want to stop yelling at their kids. These are worthy goals, but if you use those specific words, you may never successfully reach them. That's because you are focusing on the thing you don't want. Your energy will be put into the negative aspect because that's the part you are bringing up.

Simply adding the word "stop" or "lose" or "don't" or "quit" in front of the thing you don't want is highly ineffective. Remember your bouncer with your VIP list? Your bouncer has a peculiar learning disability. It can't process negative qualifiers like "stop" or "don't" so it only hears the rest of the sentence. Below are a few examples with the negative qualifiers underlined.

What you say versus what your bouncer hears:

I _don't_ yell at my kids = I yell at my kids
I eat _no_ processed sugar = I eat processed sugar
I _no longer_ have cancer = I have cancer
I _don't_ smoke = I smoke
I _don't_ need glasses = I need glasses
I am _never_ going to do that = I am going to do that

You can see how significantly your language can slow down your manifesting! I like to compare your bouncer's learning disability to a Google search. If you type into Google "Don't show me pictures of unicorns" what will every single result be? A picture of a unicorn!

Sometimes it's just as easy as saying the opposite. Like instead of I hate my job, say I love my job. Or instead of my house is a mess, say my house is clean. Other declarations need to go into more detail because there is no effective way to say the direct opposite. So how do you make something positive when it's more complicated than a quick flip?

My best tip for you is to think about how you will feel in the absence of the negative thing or circumstance. Use that picture as inspiration for new wording.

Here are some suggestions with the previous examples turned into positives:

I don't yell at my kids = I speak patiently and kindly to my kids with love and warmth
I eat no processed sugar = I honor my body by choosing healthy desserts with organic sugars
I no longer have cancer = My body is 100% healthy and whole and heals itself perfectly
I don't smoke = I breathe in only clean healthy air and my lungs are thriving
I don't need glasses = All the parts of my eyes are shaped perfectly to see clearly near and far
I am never going to do that = I do only those things that help me succeed and be happy

→ Now You Try It! ←

Take a bad habit you want to break and turn it into a positive declaration without using the negative habit in your sentence, or any other negative word like no or don't.

The third protocol is to keep your declaration Present.

When do you want your goal to happen? This week? Okay! This month? great! This year? Doable! At some vague point in the future? Nope. Because guess what? Vague points in the future NEVER become NOW. Someday is always somewhere in the future. Soon never comes. If you are not specific about the timeframe, your subconscious will make sure it never happens. Being vague about when you want something is the same thing as crossing your fingers and whispering "I don't really want this, but I'm going to pretend like I do."

Keeping your declarations in the present is one of the biggest challenges I have seen with my clients. And one of the biggest issues is that so many people are set on using the word WILL in their declarations! Will = some vague point in the future. And another danger word is CAN. Can = someday I might decide to act on the skills and desires I have, but who knows when or if I will ever get to that point.

The WORST motivational quote I have ever seen (because it totally messes with your subconscious) is the ubiquitous "I can do hard things." There are so many things wrong with this declaration. First, it uses the word can. Sure you 'can,' but when will you ever decide to? And second, it emphasizes 'hard' things. Who wants to manifest hard things?! And third, what are these unspoken 'things' you are manifesting? Are they going to help you manifest your goals? Well if they are super hard and beat you up, probably not any time soon! My favorite counter declaration for that abomination is "Everything is easy for me!" You have a choice between hard or easy - why not always choose easy?

If you want to adopt a popular saying as your declaration, please switch to something highly effective, like this gem by R. S. Grey I have been seeing a lot lately: "She believed she could, and so she did." Or even Nike's slogan "Just Do It."

The Drive-Thru Method of Manifesting

I mentioned the importance of not being vague about the time frame, so I know some of you are wondering if you need to include a deadline. The answer is yes if it helps you, no if it hinders you. Clear as mud, right? What does it mean when I say 'if it helps you or if it hinders you?' Some people are highly motivated by deadlines. Others are paralyzed by them.

You know yourself. If you will move heaven and earth to meet a deadline and it gives you energy and ideas, by all means put a deadline on that manifestation! But I have seen people who get so hung up on the deadline looming closer and closer that it totally shuts them down. The pressure causes them to make zero progress towards the thing they are trying to manifest.

So which type are you? Use that information to decide for yourself whether or not you need to add deadlines when manifesting. If you do add a deadline, and you don't make it in time, how will you handle it? The best scenario: take note that this goal is apparently going to take a little longer than planned and that's totally fine.

Keep going and do everything on your end that needs doing. When all the things happen that need to happen before it comes, it will show up - as long as you don't repel it by freaking out over deadlines being missed and focusing negative energy into the situation.

→ **Now You Try It!** ←

Practice saying your goal as a statement that you already have accomplished. Avoid the 'wills' and the 'cans' and say it like it's already part of your daily life now.

Don't Forget the G!

We have covered the 3Ps: personal, positive, and present. But there is a special protocol I like to add that doesn't start with a P. It's Gratitude. Gratitude is the secret sauce to manifesting. Without it, you may start to feel like a demanding, self-centered toddler. And that guilt will shut you down.

Adding gratitude changes the energy of your declarations. It lifts them up a notch to almost prayer-like status. Expressing gratitude for something you don't have yet is powerful! Not only is your subconscious mind tricked into thinking you've already achieved your goal so it can stop fighting you, but gratitude is a guaranteed vibration boost!

There has been scientific research done into emotions and vibrational frequencies, and if you search 'vibrational frequency chart' on the internet, you will see hundreds of color charts with all the emotions listed in order of their vibrational frequency. Shame is at the bottom, just above death. Gratitude is almost at the very top. Anytime you need to raise your vibration, just add some gratitude into your day. And to make your manifesting more powerful, add some gratitude into your declarations.

The easiest way is to simply tack on "I am so grateful..." to the beginning of a sentence. Or "I am filled with gratitude to..." Put it in a way that feels natural to you so you aren't stumbling over the words. I also like to add in an "I am so excited to..." now and then because excitement is also a higher-vibrating emotion.

→ Now You Try It! ←

Go back to the 3 practice statements you just made for each of the 3 protocols and add an element of gratitude to each one.

So now you know the 4 elements needed to make your declarations powerful:

Personal	Positive
Present	Gratitude

Later in this book I will teach you about manifestos - a full page of declarations that start with a power statement and cover each area of your dream life that you read out loud every morning.

Facebook Post on Gratitude, March 2020

You guys know that I am very dedicated to spreading the practice of gratitude. It has one of the highest vibrations of all the emotions, so it's easy to use it to get out of a funk, defuse a bad mood, and to raise yourself out of wallowing in your trials.

One of my clients told me a story last night about using gratitude that was so powerful I asked her if I could put it in my book. I realized I also need to share it here. So with her permission, I am sharing her story.

The client is a beautiful, wise, kind wife and mother who knows who she is and how to live her mission. But she suffers from occasional flare-ups of fibromyalgia that leave her nearly non-functional until the flare-up passes.

She woke up a couple days ago with an especially severe flare-up and couldn't move her ankles or hands without extreme effort and pain. She was listening to a recording of my weekly free manifesting class and heard me talking about how gratitude is such a high frequency emotion that it can totally lift you out of all the negative emotions.

She got the inspiration to speak words of gratitude into her hands. Soon she was telling each joint of each finger, and then her wrists, what she was grateful for, one by one. The warm breath of her words washed over each painful joint. Then she did it with her ankles by speaking into her hands then placing her warm hands on her ankles.

After doing her hands, her ankles, and her hands a second time, she noticed that her hands lost their pain and stiffness. She was able to get out of her comfy chair and stand up. She then did a power pose while declaring more gratitude. Soon she was pain-free and full of energy and went about her day with no physical problems.

The thing that took away her pain was gratitude. No painkillers. No hot bath. No going back to sleep. Gratitude raised the vibration of her body to the level where pain no longer could stay. She was set free from the manacles of fibromyalgia pain and lived a totally functional rest of her day. Simply from speaking gratitude into the pain.

I was so grateful that she shared this huge experience with me. And I am so grateful to have been a tiny part of that success. Gratitude is everything. Even pain relief.

TO REALLY DO
NOTHING,
WITH PERFECTION,
IS AS DIFFICULT
AS DOING
EVERYTHING.
—
ALAN WATTS

Chapter 9

Step 4: Meditation

You are so excited and filled with anticipation because you have finally decided what you'd like to eat and placed your order. The appetizing pictures of food surrounding your car are tantalizing you with their sparkling ice and dripping sauces. Now your only job is to patiently wait. You make sure to sit in silence and focus on the speaker, awaiting the instructions that you know are coming so that you can progress one step closer to receiving your delicious food.

You've just declared what you want. Meditation is the part where you listen for the answers. Or in the case of the Drive-Through analogy, this is where you leave your window rolled down, you leave your radio off, you stay off your phone, and you wait patiently. You know an answer is coming, though your hunger might make you a bit impatient. You have faith that the speaker is going to give you instructions or information that you need in order to progress in your journey to get food!

Now imagine that you've ordered food and you are sitting there in your car waiting, and you suddenly feel raindrops on your left arm. Oh! Better roll up the window! You just cut off your channel to the information you are waiting for. And then along comes a squirrel! I wonder if I got an email from that place yet? Better check my phone. Gosh, it's quiet in here. I'll just turn the radio on. Suddenly you are completely deaf and distracted and there is no way you can hear the speaker saying to you "hello? hello? are you still there?"

It seems ridiculous, right? Why would you order food then make it so you are completely incommunicado? But we do this in real life. We do this every day. We ask for help from our higher power then we run off and forget all about it. We look at our vision board and think about getting all the amazing things on it, and then we run off and forget all about it. We think about our goals and get really excited for a minute, but then we get distracted and our minds run off and forget all about it. There is a dangerous pattern here.

We don't listen. We never stop the noise around us. We don't make room for incoming messages. We are like a full voicemail box. We send out a message to someone and they try to call us with the information we need, but we don't hear the phone ring and it goes to voicemail, but then the dreaded message plays. "I'm sorry, but this user's voicemail is full." And then you wonder why nobody ever gets back to you.

Meditation is your time to clear out that voicemail box. Turn off your radio, put your phone down, stop worrying about all the things you've got to take care of today, tomorrow and next week. Let your mind clear and go into receiving mode for a few minutes after your declarations. There are ideas trying to come to you that will help you achieve your goals, so shut up and listen!

Something I really struggle with when trying to meditate is that I fall asleep if I stop and sit quietly for more than about 30 seconds. Because our bodies can translate meditation as us winding down to go to sleep, it's natural to doze off when attempting to meditate.

Here are a few things to try if you struggle with this.

Sit up straight. Don't try to meditate in bed. Get out of that comfy chair that swallows you up. Keep your back straight and just uncomfortable enough to keep you from drifting off quickly. You only need a couple minutes, so don't worry if that's all you can stay awake for.

Try a guided meditation audio. There are thousands of them on YouTube, and there are apps a-plenty! Having someone walk you through the process can be just enough distraction to keep you awake.

Do your meditation when you are feeling the most awake. If you know you drowse off at 2:30 every afternoon, don't schedule your meditation near 2:30.

Stay in a brightly lit room. I often try to meditate in my room, which is darker than the rest of the house with only one window and a giant tree outside that one window. My living room is much brighter as it faces south and has huge windows with no shade outside.

Play instrumental music that perks you up. But make sure to choose music that has no lyrics to distract you!

Remember you are just clearing out space in your mind so that you are in a state to receive ideas or instructions. You don't have to do 20 minute sessions every day - even 60 seconds is better than nothing! I frequently do only a minute or two of meditation.

Another benefit of that is that during the day when I am doing something else, an idea will come to me because I've cleared a bit of space in my brain for new input! You may not receive answers during your meditation, but you will be more able to receive them any time during your day!

I do (and recommend) a very simple process for meditation, which is as follows:

Find a quiet spot to sit down.

Set a timer for 1-10 minutes, your choice (increase your time gradually).

Close your eyes.

Place your hands on your knees, palms up and open.

Uncross your legs unless you are sitting cross-legged on the floor.

Get grounded (optional - see technique on next page)

Focus on breathing in through your nose and out through your mouth.

- Feel the air come into your lungs and don't notice anything else.
- With each breath, try to get air a little deeper into the bottom of your lungs.
- Slow down and make each breath last a little longer.
- When a squirrel thought comes, thank it, release it, and go back to your breathing.
- When the timer goes off, come back to reality and jot down any ideas you get.

Grounding

Though not required, it is very helpful to ground yourself when meditating. You are inviting your higher power to be more involved in your meditation, which can benefit you greatly. Here is a great way to get grounded:

Imagine a bright white beam of light coming down from your higher power to just above your head. It enters the top of your head and lights up every cell of your body as it passes through you. It then passes through the floor, the ground, the layers of the earth, all the way to the molten core of the earth.

As this light shines through you, it cleans out all your doubts, fears, distractions, and anything else that isn't pure, unconditional love. You are connected to your higher power above, and mother earth below, and you can draw upon the powers of both to nurture and nourish you. All negativity is instantly washed away as soon as you notice it. Your mind opens and your heart is filled with love and light. You can now see things that you need to see, know things that you need to know, and feel things that you need to feel. All in the safety of that pure, white light coursing through your body.

When your meditation timer goes off, release the light but notice that a portion of it stays with you in your heart, and your mind stays open to receive inspiration throughout the day.

→ Now You Try It! ←

Practice getting grounded. It gets easier with practice. Set the intention that you are going to succeed and follow the steps I laid out on the previous two pages.

TRUST YOURSELF,
YOU KNOW MORE
THAN YOU THINK
YOU DO.

—

DR. BENJAMIN
SPOCK

Chapter 10

Step 5: Inspiration

Suddenly a voice comes out of the speaker box, startling you out of your silent contemplation. You jump! Then you focus on the voice. It's saying that they just ran out of teriyaki chicken and would you like to substitute another kind of chicken, or try the teriyaki steak instead. You were not expecting this. You have to make another decision, but you can do it! Teriyaki steak it is! The voice then gives you your total and tells you to pull up to the first window. Yes! Food is almost here!

The next step in the manifesting formula is inspiration. This is the step where you receive instruction. If you don't do the previous step to clear out your overfilled brain, you won't be able to receive instruction.

Once again, imagine you are in the drive-thru lane and you've been eagerly awaiting the instructions to tell you your next step in receiving food. You hear them say a total and then they give you your action step. That step requires some kind of action on your part. Usually it's to pull up to the 1st window, or more likely, the 2nd window. (What ever happened to all those 1st windows that now sit abandoned and empty?)

Inspiration sounds simple enough, right? But for many it's not. Why do some of us have trouble receiving answers from within? Or from our higher power? Or the universe? I used to struggle really badly with recognizing ideas when they came to me. And I see people struggling with it all around me. We have become a society of second-guessers.

One reason I was such a second-guesser was because I listened to everyone except my higher power and my inner voice. I didn't trust my own ability to differentiate between crazy stupid ideas and actual inspiration. I was scared that anything I tried would be wrong and probably even end in disaster.

As a kid I was inadvertently taught that I couldn't ever say no, and therefore my opinion didn't matter. When your opinion doesn't matter, what difference does it make what ideas you come up with, right? Whether by guilt trips or spankings, I think a lot of us are raised believing that our voice doesn't matter because we can't use it to say "no."

Another reason I had trouble is that I am a recovering people pleaser. I absolutely could not handle disappointing anyone, ever! Because other people's opinions of me mattered more than my own. And other people's wants and needs mattered more than my own. I couldn't bear to do anything that might make someone not approve of me.

One of the hardest things I have had to deal with is not being liked by everyone. I still struggle with that one sometimes but now it's on a whole new level - as I put myself out there in the public eye more and more I now have to deal with strangers who don't like me or my message. It hurts to see negative comments on my posts that are spreading positivity. And I've only had a few of those.

I don't know how famous people handle their haters, but that is super tough on our need to be loved and accepted. Not worrying about what people think about you is easier said than done, but it's a worthy goal to work towards.

Factors like these build up over time to destroy your confidence in yourself and your ideas. When you can't move forward with conviction, you are likely to stagnate. I stagnated for years. It's not a good place to be.

I cycled through the same pattern over and over again. Try something, get negative feedback and positive feedback, obsess over the negative feedback, go into hiding, slowly build up enough courage (and time to forget pain), and then try something new. That was my life until I learned a seemingly crazy strategy that taught me to start trusting myself and my ideas.

The strategy is this: assume EVERY idea that comes to you is amazing and will propel you forward if you act upon it. Believe that your mind is capable of showing you only fantastic ideas and therefore, every idea you come up with must be fantastic. I started doing every idea that came to me after my meditation process, no matter what. This was hard at first, but it started to become easy and eventually it became automatic. I stopped questioning myself and my ideas. I decided that if my brain came up with an idea, knowing my goals and wanting me to succeed, it's going to be a good idea.

The funny thing is that often my plan of action morphs into a completely different action as I find myself swerving during execution of said plan. Sometimes it turns out that I just needed to take ANY action to get access to my higher level ideas.

Yes, I believe that your brain has levels of ideas. When you always push aside and argue with the level 1 ideas, your brain never even bothers to give you the level 2 ideas. It knows you aren't serious and doesn't want to waste the better ideas on your non-action-taking self.

And don't even dream about getting a level 3 idea! You aren't remotely ready for a level 3 idea if you still bat away your level 1 ideas.

→ Now You Try It! ←

For those of you who can't trust the ideas you get yet, here is a helpful exercise. Each time you do the formula and you've just finished the meditation step, get a paper and pen and write down every single idea that comes to you, no matter how crazy or illegal or unethical.

Don't worry, you're not going to act on those, but you do need to write them all down. When you're all out of ideas, go through your list. Cross out all the ones that would put you in jail or cause harm to yourself or your loved ones. Cross out anything else that is questionable or dangerous.

You now have a list of reasonable, doable ideas with which you are going to create a chart. Your chart will have the following columns, from left to right (see next page):

Date Received, Idea, Date Completed, Result
Rate it (Good, Neutral, Bad)

This chart will be one that you use for at least a month to build evidence that you can trust yourself and your inspiration. (If you would like a copy of my form, please go to http://bit.ly/IdeaChart to download a PDF of the form I created for myself.) Seeing the results of acting on your ideas will completely change your way of thinking about yourself. You will gain self-confidence as you watch the evidence grow that you have good ideas.

Idea Chart

Date	Idea	Done	Result	Rating
				+ or -
				+ or -
				+ or -
				+ or -
				+ or -
				+ or -
				+ or -
				+ or -
				+ or -
				+ or -
				+ or -
				+ or -
				+ or -
				+ or -
				+ or -
				+ or -
				+ or -
				+ or -

Idea Chart

Date	Idea	Done	Result	Rating
				+ or -
				+ or -
				+ or -
				+ or -
				+ or -
				+ or -
				+ or -
				+ or -
				+ or -
				+ or -
				+ or -
				+ or -
				+ or -
				+ or -
				+ or -
				+ or -
				+ or -
				+ or -

Whatever you think you can do, or believe you can do... begin it, because action has magic, grace and power in it.

—

Johann Wolfgang von Goethe

Chapter 11

Step 6: Implementation

You've been told what to do, so now you do it! Pull forward to the second window and pay the person standing there! All you have to do is lift your foot off the brake, idle forward until you reach that window, then put your foot back down on the brakes. Hand the person at the window your cash or card, take back whatever they hand you, then reach for the big sack of food they hold out towards you! Success! You have received food! You have just completed all six steps of the drive-thru formula and it worked perfectly - you have got dinner in your hands!

Time for action!! This is where things get exciting! Or some of you might lean towards using the word 'scary' instead. I totally understand the fear that comes up during this step, but research has proven that the exact same chemicals are dumped into your bloodstream whether you feel 'scared' or 'excited' because they are nearly the same emotion. The only practical difference is the name you give it - so name it Excitement!

If you were in a drive-thru, this is the step where you finally receive your food! You've decided where to go, visualized the food you want, declared out loud the food you'd like to eat, stopped talking and waited quietly, received instructions, and now you act on those instructions to receive your food. (And if you were ravenously hungry, the first 5 steps might seem like they took forever.) You've done it! This is the whole reason you were in the drive-thru! The denouement! The climax! The main attraction! At last, food!!

Looking back, is there any step you could have left out and still arrived at this point where you are pulling up to a window and a lovely person leans out with a bag of food for you? No. All the steps are required to get you to this point. This glorious point in the process is what we call success, or manifesting, or living your dreams.

Well, only if you properly execute this final step. Step 6 is (if you remember my spoiler at the beginning of this book) probably the most often missed step.

So many people reach this step and instead of taking their next inspired step (which in the Drive-Thru Method is paying and getting their food), they decide to do something else, or do nothing at all. They just leave without a word and without food. But how could someone not pull up to the window and get their food, you may ask? How could they go through all that work and then just drive away without taking that hot, delicious bag of goodies?

If you were literally in a drive-thru there are several reasons I can think of that would cause you to abort your food-procuring mission.

Maybe your spouse called and said the bank account was overdrawn and asked you to not spend any money today. Maybe you reached for your wallet and realized you left it on the roof of your car when you were getting gas 10 minutes ago. Maybe your kids called and said they found a coupon for a totally different drive-thru and they will be so happy if you go to that one instead, especially because it just launched toys from the huge kids movie in theaters right now. Maybe you've been holding it and you literally can't wait another second before you have an accident in your new car and there's a bathroom across the street. Totally feasible reasons to drive away and abandon your food, right?

But what about real life. Would you ever do that with your goals? Would you invest your time and energy into the manifesting formula, doing all the steps to make your goal happen, and then get an inspired action step that just makes you say, 'Never mind" and walk away?

It happens all the time. I have seen clients do it over and over again. I've done it myself over and over again! Why? Why would we do that to ourselves? The easy answer is fear of success. The deeper answer is that your subconscious mind has a 'worst case scenario' story tucked away in a place you can't normally access. This hidden story is like a horror movie that ends in death, abandonment, betrayal and more. And because you can't access it easily, you don't even know it's there.

You are completely unaware that your subconscious mind has a secret prime directive to stop you from reaching that goal by any means necessary.

To you it looks like self-sabotage, people triggering you, getting sick at the worst time, mandatory overtime at work, the dog chewing up your laptop, or any other 'random' thing that derails and distracts you from your objective. But what is really happening is that your subconscious is actively attracting disasters to keep you preoccupied and distracted so you forget your goal, or get discouraged about it, or run out of time or energy to accomplish it.

It might seem like there is no way around your subconscious, but there is. You have the power to create a 'best case scenario' to replace the 'worst case scenario.'

How to find the horror story lurking in your subconscious

You can do this alone or have someone help you. My mentor, Kirk Duncan, taught me this process and walked me through it the first time. It goes a little bit like an interview. You need to answer the following questions:

What is your goal?
What needs to happen for you to reach your goal?
What is keeping you from doing those things?
What would happen if you overcame those excuses and did it anyway?

What happens if THAT happens?
And what happens if THAT happens?
And then what happens?
Then what?
Where does it lead in the end?

When I first did this with Kirk, my answers revealed that my story ended in suicide. And I was shocked. I had no idea that I had this completely irrational fear hidden in the shadows, running my life. It seemed ridiculous! But fear is powerful, and unacknowledged fear is even more powerful.

When we got to the rock bottom, Kirk told me that now I get to write a new 'best case scenario' to address every single step of that journey to despair I had just unearthed. It wasn't easy. My subconscious fought me. First, it made me do a half-ass job at it. Then it made me embarrassed by it so I didn't want to read it. But I fought through and I rewrote it and now it's incredible. I even recorded myself reading it WITH ENTHUSIASM (not always easy) so when I hear it, I get an emotional response. Usually I giggle at how much I got into it, but giggles raise your vibration.

I listened to it many times a day, especially when waking up and going to sleep, and any time I woke up in the night. And it changed my horror story. Suddenly new opportunities started appearing. New ideas came and I executed them immediately. New people showed up in my life. My old story got laid off and the new story took over. Action steps became easier and less scary. My comfort zone grew, and I started manifesting much better things.

→ Now You Try It! ←

Interview yourself or have someone you trust ask you the questions. Find your hidden horror story and rewrite it. Address every step and fear all the way down so that your new story is just as long and detailed as your old one.

Blog Post After My First Time on Stage Speaking

That Fateful Facebook Finger err... Thumb

I saw a 'like' on Facebook in October that caught my eye. One of my friends liked an event held by a group called SpeakUp – The Professional Speakers Studio. I had recently started harboring secret dreams of being a public speaker like my spirit animal, Brene Brown, so I clicked on the event. It had 3 things going for it: it was about getting better as a public speaker, it was happening soon, and it was less than an hour's drive away. So I bought a ticket!

The day of the event I got all cute and headed up to Sandy. I got out of my car at the venue and braced myself. As I shakily entered the building a very sweet and friendly woman greeted me and checked me in. I was scared to venture past her and approach the meeting area full of strangers who I assumed were all professional speakers. Who was I to just waltz in there and think I could become a speaker? I had just barely started my journey of transformation and felt totally unworthy to be there. But I really wanted to be there. So I had to force myself to walk in and sit down at a table of strangers.

Feeling Like a Fraud

Thoughts of inadequacies danced through my head as I sat there totally alone at a table full of people. They all seemed to know each other, and I felt like an exposed rabbit under a sky of circling hawks. Just as I was about to bolt, I turned to the people on my left and blurted out "Hey guys, I'm really scared and I feel like I'm going to leave, so please help me stay!"

My inner voice was screaming "NOOO! WHY DID I SAY THAT?" but those people were amazing and kind and they instantly befriended me and gave me the support I needed to keep my terror-filled bum in that chair. I soon found out that many of them were highly successful professional speakers and even had written books. Somehow I started to shift from feeling like a delusional party crasher to feeling blessed to be learning from them.

Best Advice Ever: Just Leap!

I asked one of them, Kris Barney, how she got started. She told me that when she decided she wanted to be a speaker, she JUST LEAPT. She created her own opportunities to speak and then showed up. Then she invited me to take my own leap. I filed that challenge away to ponder later and sat back to enjoy the event.

That day's meeting featured a speaking competition called The Message – which is kind of a cross between The Voice and a Ted Talk. The four contestants spoke for 10 minutes each, then the three judges gave them very insightful feedback. After the last speaker, the judges left to deliberate and soon came back in to announce the winner. It was all very exciting.

What On Earth Was I Thinking?

At the end of the event they announced that they would be doing The Message again next month and that there was one spot left. I immediately started listing the reasons why it would be insane for me to sign up for that last spot. I was just there to check things out. I've never spoken anywhere before. I had nothing to say. Who would even want to hear me speak? It was ridiculous to even consider it. Who was I to just declare myself a speaker? Wasn't there some kind of official process you have to go through to get certified or something? Didn't someone need to give me permission first? Who did I think I was?

Reluctantly agreeing with myself, I got up and said goodbye and headed out. Then I decided to go to the bathroom because it's almost an hour to my house. As I sat on the toilet (probably TMI here, sorry) I started to argue with myself. Why not give a try? What's it going to hurt? I won't get arrested or booed or pummeled with rotten tomatoes. Don't I want to be a speaker? This is the perfect beginning. It's been dropped into my lap. Be brave. Speakers are brave. Do it. Remember what Kris Barney said. Just leap.

Bravery Takes Over – But Looks Like Crazy!

By the time I was done in there and opened the bathroom door with a paper towel-clad hand, I had decided to go see if that spot was left.
I went up to the emcee, Cary White, and said "Is that 4th spot still open?"

He said it was. I said "I need to take that spot."
And then I burst into tears.

He said "You don't have to do it! It's just for those who want to. It's not required." Through my tears I said "Yes, I have to do it." He said "So you want the spot?" I said "No. But I have to take it." I could feel the crazy alarms going off in his mind. But he was steadfast in the face of my bi-polar breakdown.

"Well, we'd love to hear from you!" The look on his face told me that he was expecting a total stage fright disaster. The sweet woman who had checked me in brought the paper over and I got officially signed up to speak at the next event, which was in a month. I cried all the way to my car and halfway home. Tears of joy that I had actually done it. Tears of terror that I now had to do it. Tears of discomfort at stretching my comfort zone. Tears of hope that I might actually become the next Brene Brown. =D

Two Months To Pull It All Together Three Times

I had my talk written within 4 days. I wanted to be completely ready with it totally memorized. And then the next event was canceled. I was given the option to still speak at the December event and I said yes. So suddenly I had a whole extra month to work on it. I ended up rewriting it several times and ended up with 3 different talks by the time December 14 rolled around. Which turned out to be a good thing.

The event started out great with lots of energy and excitement and I wasn't even scared. I mingled and chatted and met lots of new people. They gave each speaker a number and then made slips of paper with our numbers and drew them out of a 'hat' (no actual hats were used) to see who went first. When it came time to draw, I started to feel the nerves slowly creep in. The first name called was... NOT ME!

The Speaking Begins

So I sat back and listened to Jerry Lund tell about his experience with being a fire chief, then becoming temporarily disabled, losing his job, and dealing with the aftermath. The judges gave him great feedback, then the next speaker was drawn. This time it was... STILL NOT ME!

I started to feel the pressure big time so I escaped to the bathroom for a minute or two. When I came back I listened to Luke Watkins finish his talk about overcoming his addiction by using tools like gratitude and service. And that's when I panicked. He just gave my talk. Then I remembered that I had written 3 different talks. No problem! I'll just give one of the other 2 talks!

My First Time Speaking On a Stage

So when they drew the next name – it WAS me! As I walked up to the stage, Cary told the story of my tear-filled request to speak and was probably worried that I would spend my 10 minutes staring blankly at the judges in a catatonic state. I climbed up the stairs and crossed to the middle of the stage, grabbing the mic on my way. I stood in the blinding spotlight and proclaimed "This has been the best year of my life." I hadn't written that into any of my talks. But I ran with it. I ended up making a patchwork creation of all 3 of my talks that I think was better than any of my previous ones.

I surprised myself. I actually enjoyed speaking. I made people laugh. I had audience participation. I felt comfortable and relaxed and energized and loved. The feedback was valuable. Move more. Say 'um' less. Go deeper into the sadness before you tell us how you get yourself out of it. Maintain eye contact. They also told me how great I did, how funny I was, how vulnerable and honest my stories were. I was euphoric.

I Leaped – and I Liked It (Spoiler Alert – I WON!)

After me, there was one more speaker. Hilary Bagley told us about her amazing conversation with God and the concept of "What if you are doing everything exactly right already?" We then waited while the judges left the room to pick a winner. When they came back and announced that the winner was...

ME!, I was stunned. Bobby Glen James told me to stand up and take a bow, so I did. Then I threw my arms in the air and whooped.

Could being a speaker actually exist in my realm of possibility? I think YES! And now I have one year to get really great at it, and then compete in the finale with each of the other monthly winners! Plus, I am speaking at my first actual event next month. For real. And I'm emceeing the event too! All this because I leaped!

If you see something that you want to pursue and your fear is holding you back, let me just pass on to you that invitation that Kris Barney gave me. JUST LEAP!

WITHIN ALL OF
US IS A DIVINE
CAPACITY TO
MANIFEST AND
ATTRACT ALL
THAT WE NEED
AND DESIRE.
—
WAYNE DYER

Chapter 12

Speed Manifesting

You don't ALWAYS have to be super scientific about the formula. You can use it on the fly, without getting deep into formalities. As long as some form of each step is involved, you can manifest quickly with a casual adherence to the formula. In other words, sometimes you can do an impromptu version of manifesting that doesn't have to be so formal. I like to call this Speed Manifesting. Some of my best manifesting has been done this way!

The speed manifesting that you probably do all the time: the parking spot!

One thing that I know everyone loves to manifest is a great parking spot. And in my years of teaching manifesting, that is the most common success story I hear from audiences. They love picturing that perfect spot on the front row that just serendipitously is there for them when they pull up to the grocery store. When you do that, you are using the formula casually.

You don't sit and visualize or use the 3 Ps or listen for your next step. You leave the house headed for your destination without even thinking about your parking spot. But when you get close to the store, you start imagining yourself finding that magical empty spot. You mention it out loud if you have someone in the car with you, and you are filled with anticipation and certainty. You arrive just seconds after someone has pulled out, but before anyone else shows up. Then you cheer and laugh or feel a wave of contentment that says all is right with the world. That is speed manifesting!

Speed Manifesting As A Team

My family loves to walk along the river together, and when the weather is even remotely nice, we make it part of our daily routine. Recently we were headed for the trail in the evening and it was fairly cold, so my husband was wearing a hoodie with one of those big pouches that go across the front instead of regular pockets. When we got out of the car he dropped his keys into the big pouch instead of putting his keys in his jeans pocket.

Moments after we started, our dog needed to, uh, do his business. My son and I walked on as my husband waited for Cooper to finish. He bagged up the evidence and chucked it in the park trash can and then ran across the huge grassy area to catch up with us on the paved trail. We had a lovely evening on the river trail and finally headed back towards the car. The sun had gone down and as we approach the car it is rapidly turning dark.

We reach the car and the street lights come on. My husband rummages around in his pockets and says, "Kelly, did I give you the car keys?" I tell him that he hadn't, but I check my pockets anyway. We start to get alarmed as he searches his pockets again, but no keys. We turn on our phone flashlights and search through the windows of the car for any sign of the keys. We can't find them anywhere.

I call my neighbor and ask her if she's home. She is out running errands so on her way home she goes by my house and grabs a spare key off the hook. She drives over to the park with our precious spare key and we thank her profusely. We get in the car, look for the keys some more, to no avail, then drive home.

We decide that in the morning, as soon as the sun comes up, we will go search the park. My husband is fairly certain that his running across the big grassy part of the park to catch up with us caused the keys to bounce out of the side of his hoodie's pouch. Which means that our search can be pretty targeted in that area.

Before we go to bed, he draws a picture of himself holding his newly-found keys. He's taking a course where he has to draw his intention for the next day, so that was the natural choice for his nightly drawing. This is where he starts using the manifesting formula to find his keys. Setting that intention is like doing the first 2 steps of the manifesting formula - he got clear on what he wanted, and he visualized it happening.

Morning comes and it is raining. It's also pitch black because of the cloud cover. And snow is in the forecast for 7am - 20 minutes before sunrise. We realize we are going to be searching in the dark with rain and possibly snow if we don't find the keys right away. So we bundle up and start talking about how grateful we are that we found the keys so quickly. Which was step 3 of the formula - declaration: say it out loud.

We grab some flashlights and get in the car. On the way to the park I say a prayer and first I ask for directions on how and where to look, then I express gratitude for finding them. I assume in the prayer that we had already found them. Then I wait for ideas to come into my head. I get one! A flash of a news story I once saw of a search and rescue in the woods. The search team maps out zig zag lines across a search area and has everyone walking side by side so no ground is missed. It's all very systematic and intentional. So there is step 4 and 5 - meditate and receive inspiration.

The park is pitch black as we pull into the parking lot, but when we step out of the car, the parking lot lights come on! They light up the first 20 feet of the grassy area which helps us immensely! I tell my husband my plan, but first we decide to walk the way he thought he ran and search that path first. No keys. We head back to the beginning and start our systematic zig zag. We talk about how happy we are that we found the keys. We do one zig, then a zag.

Just as we start our 3rd my husband yells "MY KEYS!" Sure enough, there they are - right at the beginning of our next zig. We gasp and laugh and whoop excitedly. My husband grabs them and says "Let's say a prayer of thanks!" We go back to the car, get in, and both say a gratitude prayer.

That was a great example of how you can speed manifest. Sometimes you just need to manifest something right now - and that is what it could look like. You still follow all the steps of the formula, but you do them quickly and passionately! Notice that my husband did 2 of the steps and I did 2 of the steps, and we did the remaining 2 steps together. We manifested these keys being found as a team. That is important to know - when you are manifesting as a team, you can each do some of the steps yourself, and do some together. As long as the team is getting some form of all 6 steps in, it doesn't matter who is doing which step.

Speed Manifesting Money

I have a client who wanted to manifest $12,000 in less than a week for something very fun and important. She decided to take the manifesting formula on a wild ride - she set her phone alarm to go off every two hours all day long. When her alarm sounded, she did the manifesting formula, including the action step. After 2 days of doing a new action step every 2 hours, that $12,000 showed up and she got to do the thing she was so excited about doing.

Move out of your comfort zone. You can only grow if you are willing to feel awkward and uncomfortable when you try something new.

—

Brian Tracy

Chapter 13

Stretching Your Comfort Zone

I was taught by several different mentors that everything I want is outside of my comfort zone. And that not ever getting what you really want isn't that comfortable after all. So there goes my comfort zone! The comfort inside your comfort zone is a consolation prize. It's 2nd place. It's 'good enough' when you could have 'great' or even better than great.

For some people, that is acceptable. Having what they've always had, doing what they've always done, and getting as far as they've already gone is sufficient for them. And that's ok. You are not one of those people.

You are not satisfied to stay at your current level for the next 50 years and never push yourself to achieve something spectacular. You are not happy with sitting around watching TV and keeping your blinders on while convincing yourself that it's too scary to reach for your dreams.

Your comfort zone is itching to be stretched! It is too confining, too complacent, and too boring. You are in the exciting, innovative category of humans with a growth mindset.

Without you, humanity never progresses. Without you, the world never knows it's ok to take a risk because growth is worth any risk of failure.

And really, there is no such a thing as failure except for failing to try. Because if you try and don't succeed, you've still had a success. You have learned a thing that doesn't work, so you can adjust and try again. That is a success.

If you try again, and miss your target again, then you have again learned something new which will help you reach your goal next time, or the time after that, or the time after that. You are always learning, adjusting, and trying again until you reach your target. There is no such thing as failure unless you never try at all.

I sometimes secretly think to myself that my favorite hobby is stretching my comfort zone. I often like to see scary obstacles as something to be conquered instead of something to be avoided. Not always - yet. But often. And that used to be 'never,' so 'often' is a huge leap. Which means that the desire to stretch your comfort zone can be grown and nurtured. You don't have to be born with the desire. You can develop it just like any other skill.

Facebook Post

Asking Strangers for a Dollar

Today my business coach gave me a terrifying assignment. She made me agree to do it before she would tell me what it was. I always do everything scary she tells me to do, so I didn't think she needed to take those measures, but it was definitely the scariest thing I have ever done.

The assignment was to go to a store tonight and ask 10 strangers for a dollar. It didn't matter whether they gave me any money or not – only that I was able to make myself approach a total stranger and ask.

You might think that doesn't sound so scary, but I have never been more scared in my life. I considered giving up after I'd done a full sweep of the store and not gotten up the nerve to approach one person.

My sweet husband had come in the store with me for moral support but stayed away from me. When I went to report to him that I couldn't do it, I dissolved into tears. Luckily he thinks my business coach is the biggest genius ever, so instead of letting me escape my doom, he gave me a pep talk. He said that I needed to do it, and now the tears would probably make people more likely to actually give me a dollar.

While that wasn't the point of the exercise, I did see his point that I would be more sympathetic if I were crying. So, I stopped crying and dried my face off. No cheating for me! I wandered off to the clothing section because people were stationary for a while, picking up pieces of clothing and unfolding them to see what they look like, then folding them back up and replacing them on the stack.

I planted my sights on a guy in his 20s shopping alone in a strange outfit and headed towards him. I said, "Excuse me, do you have a dollar I could borrow?" He politely and uncomfortably said no, and I told him it was ok, smiled and walked away. I saw another person shopping alone and tried again, only this time I didn't chicken out and say 'borrow.' She was in her 40s, dressed up like an 80's jazzercizer (today was Halloween) looking at books. When I said 'excuse me' to her, she immediately backed up thinking she was in my way. Then I said, "Do you have a dollar I could have?" and she also politely and uncomfortably said no. I smiled and said it was ok and moved on.

The Drive-Thru Method of Manifesting

The next few people were a blur, but one of them gave me my first dollar. One older woman and one man. Then a cute old grandpa in red flannel plaid gave me a $5 dollar bill. I started to get some spring in my step and I noticed that I was smiling more and sending out less apologetic energy. I started having a little fun with it. I approached a whole family and the dad said yes, and a sour-looking couple that said no. A beautiful blonde woman in her 20s heard the exchange and came towards me with a dollar in her hand and said "Do you need a dollar?"

By this point I was feeling pretty confident and I asked a whole family of 5 who said no. Then I went to the tables up front and asked another big family. The husband was slightly angry and asked why I was asking him for money. My coach had forbidden me from telling people, but since he asked me point blank, I admitted it was an experiment my coach was making me do. He growled "Well, then NO!" His wife, who was dressed as Winnie the Pooh grabbed her purse defiantly and pulled out a dollar and handed it to me and said, "Go buy some honey with this."

By the end of the adventure I had asked 11 different people/groups for a dollar and ended up with 6 "yes", 5 "no", and 11 dollars. What did I learn from this?

The prettier people all gave me money. When I smiled and was happy, people gave me money more enthusiastically. When I was awkward and embarrassed, I got more rejections. Sometimes when one spouse said no, the other jumped in and said yes. I felt braver to ask men than women. The oldest one I asked gave me 5 times what the younger ones gave me. When I asked in awkwardness, those people avoided my eyes when I saw them again in the store. When I got to 11 asks and 11 dollars, I kind of wanted to keep going! The awesome success energy is very contagious and motivating. The awkward failure energy is very sticky and disempowering.

The whole point of this exercise was to get some rejections under my belt so that I would feel more comfortable with it when it happens. It worked. And now I know how to get rejected less often: smile and be excited for the outcome, whatever it may be. Because either way, I've done my part and stretched my comfort zone, and I am equally happy with a "no" that teaches me what I need to learn, or a "yes" that leads to a sale and a transformation.

→ Now You Try It! ←

You don't have to do something as painfully stretchy as the "Asking Strangers for a Dollar" exercise, but it would be very effective to create your own comfort zone stretching exercises.

Choose your favorite goal that you are currently working on. Get in a comfy position, close your eyes, and focus on deep breathing for about a minute. Then ask yourself "What can I do in the next 24 hours to give my comfort zone a little stretch towards my goal?"

Sit quietly and listen for the answer. Some of you will get the answer as soon you start asking the question. Some of you could be waiting awhile for your intuition to kick in. Just keep breathing and thinking about reaching your goal and a step will come to you.

When you get the answer, get up and do it immediately if at all possible. If not, make sure to do it within 24 hours. Procrastination is the enemy when trying to stretch your comfort zone!

EVERYTHING IS ENERGY. MATCH THE FREQUENCY OF THE REALITY YOU WANT, AND YOU CANNOT HELP BUT GET THAT REALITY. IT CAN BE NO OTHER WAY. THIS IS NOT PHILOSOPHY. THIS IS PHYSICS.

—

ALBERT EINSTEIN

Chapter 14

Vibrational Frequency Affects Everything

Every person, animal, and object is vibrating. Though they all seem stationary when looking at them, every single thing has a vibrational frequency. It is not a theory or sci-fi or wishful thinking - it is a scientifically observed fact. Literally everything in existence has a vibrational frequency. We all emit an oscillating electrical field that is perceived as a vibration. Some things have a much higher vibrational frequency than others, and some have a much lower one.

You are a giant orchestra of vibrations. Your cells have their own vibration, your thoughts have their own vibration, your emotions have their own vibrations, and your language has its own vibration. And all of them shift up and down the vibrational scale all day long.

They are all affected by vibrations of the things you choose to consume - the food you eat, the beverages you drink, the medications you take, the music you listen to, the shows you watch, the air you breathe, the products you put on your skin, and anything else that literally enters your body in any way. They are ALSO affected by the things around you. Your belongings, your clutter, your family, your roommates, your neighbors, your pets, your yard, your books, your electronic devices, and on and on.

Why does this matter? Just like the 2 ends of magnets that can't be pushed together because they so strongly repel each other, if you want something that is vibrating at a drastically different frequency than you are, you can never attract it at your current frequency. Or in other words, the you that you are today would repel the you that you would be with that goal achieved.

Future you has progressed to a higher frequency that is in alignment with living at a level where that goal is a natural fit. Currently, you can see that possibility, get excited about it, and visualize it. But the current 'you' can't manifest it yet. As you do the manifesting formula every day, you will get an action step that leads you closer to your goal and changes your vibration.

If your vibration is drastically lower than that of your goal, then many of your action steps will be dedicated just to raising your vibration. If you can raise your vibration at the same time as working on your goal, you will be able to reach your goal faster. Your inspired action steps will be more for progress and movement instead of raising your vibration.

Working on your vibration in tandem with doing the manifesting formula is like adding fertilizer to your garden. Everything will happen faster and on a bigger scale.

There are many ways to raise your vibration. You can focus on improving what you consume, improving your surroundings, improving your thoughts, improving your emotions, improving your language, and more. To help you understand this concept better, imagine that your vibration is like your credit score.

We have an average credit score based on our debt ratio, payment history, and age of accounts. It is ALWAYS better to have a higher credit score. You get all kinds of perks. You get pre-approved for credit cards with super low interest rates. You get approved for car loans, also with great interest rates. You get approved for lots of things you probably don't even realize, like lower insurance rates, lower mortgage rates, lower security deposits and more.

Your vibration is like your energetic credit score. When your vibration is high, you get 'approved' for better things - meaning you match the criteria needed to achieve or receive those things. Imagine treating your vibration like your credit score - guarding it, nurturing it, tracking it, never doing things that might lower it, avoiding dings at all cost. What does it look like to work on protecting and increasing your vibration?

First, try improving what you consume - both with your eyes and your ears.

This was one of the first things I worked on when I learned about manifesting and how important my vibration was. Especially books and movies. I used to be a horror film junkie - nothing super bloody or supernatural, but I loved a good little scare occasionally. And I loved to read books with lots of murders, investigations, monsters, and scary creatures.

The vibration of those images and scenes was not conducive to me raising my vibration to a new, higher level. They were exciting and got my adrenaline pumping, but there was enough dark, low vibration going on that I was starting to feel the difference. I could tell when I watched or read something of that vibration, my personal vibration would dip. And since I was actively working on raising it, I realized that I needed to give up those kinds of books and movies.

Objectively assess the books, movies, TV shows, videos, etc. that you consume on a regular basis. Are they in alignment with the vibration you need to have in order to attain your goal? If not, decide if they are really worth the ding to your vibration.

Second, try improving your emotional responses.

Getting triggered by people and situations is a normal part of life. Sometimes we just get really upset and need to feel the anger. But we don't have to let it rule us, and we don't have to let it linger for minutes, hours, days, or for some people - years. Negative emotions happen for a reason - they are teaching you what you don't like. Which lets you make room in your life for more things that you do like.

Negative emotions have their place and purpose, but too often we wallow in them. We can even get so used to them that we almost prefer them, because they feel familiar.

But living with negative emotions comes with a steep price. They cost you your health. They cost you your goals. They cost you your healthy relationships. They cost you your clarity. The costs outweigh the benefits so heavily that it would seem obvious to everyone that negative emotions just aren't worth it. But you can get so entangled with your emotions that you can't see any other way.

That is exactly how I felt four years ago. I was so full of negative emotions that I didn't see a way out. For a natural optimist, that was a living hell for me.

When I learned about vibration and that I could affect it myself by choosing my own emotions, the practice of keeping a daily gratitude list became my magic weapon against the negativity. What you focus on grows - and as I focused on things to be grateful for, the things that caused my negative emotional responses faded away.

I became more aware of the positive things in my life and the negative things either shrunk or lost their power. Which is why my number one assignment with any client struggling with negativity is to make a gratitude list every day.

Gratitude is one of the highest vibrating emotions, and therefore it has the power to raise your emotional vibration faster than anything else for most people.

My favorite way to get people excited about gratitude is the 'gratirant.' This is a process I invented with my husband where we start taking turns, as quickly as we can, stating something we are grateful for. I always start with air conditioning, since I am extremely averse to being uncomfortably hot! It's become a joke now, but I still almost always start with it. We get going and build up a positive energy that just takes over and we both end up laughing and full of joy. It's amazingly powerful, and I highly recommend it to everyone!

Third, try improving your surroundings with these three strategies.

A. Start small. Eventually you will want to clean up and organize your entire home, but just start with your easiest room. For me, it's the living room. Then the bathroom, then the kitchen, then my bedroom, then my office. I say to start with your easiest room because cleaning and organizing an entire house can be overwhelming for most people. But even cleaning one corner of one room will raise your vibration. I have a friend who does her house cleaning on Mondays and she has noticed that she is always in a better mood on Mondays. It's because she is regularly raising her vibration by cleaning her house that day.

B. Tackle your clutter. Every piece of clutter in your home has its own low vibration that adds up to a big problem. I know it's really hard for some people to address their clutter because it can be overwhelming to the point of paralysis. Try with just one box of stuff, and give yourself a whole week to go through it. Baby steps are better than no steps. As you decrease the amount of clutter in your life, you will gain clarity, make room for better things, and raise your vibration significantly.

C. Choose one room to always be clean and tidy. This has been a great solution for my family. We make a united effort to keep our living room clean and it has been pretty successful. We know that we can always sit in there for a peaceful, calm feeling. We have no TV in there, so that especially keeps it serene and special. We keep a shelf of self-help books, along with inspirational art on the walls. And we all know to pick up our stuff from that room and not leave it lying around for long. What room in your house could be your special sanctuary where the vibration is noticeably higher than the rest of your house?

Fourth, try living closer to your higher power.

Your best, highest self vibrates at an exponentially higher frequency than your current self. Connecting with your higher power is an effective way to connect with your best, highest self. You want to have her in your head as much as possible because she is your ultimate goal.

One of my favorite and most effective ways to get closer to my higher power is to get out into nature. We live 2 miles from a river with a well-kept trail alongside it that we visit several times a week. We often stop and talk to a tree, sit and watch the river while listening to the rushing water, and enjoy all the sunshine, breezes, and wildlife.

Another way to connect to your higher power is to meditate. Meditation alone will raise your vibration simply because you are shutting off the constant inner chatter that is always going on in your head. But it also helps you gain control over your thoughts and emotions so that you are more open to hearing inspiration from your source.

I like to compare your mind to a full voicemail box. You're getting messages from your higher power all the time, but your voicemail is full so they can't get through to you. Meditating is a quick, easy way to delete your old voicemail and make room for new messages. You don't need a fancy process or an app on your phone to meditate - just sit comfortably with your eyes closed and focus only on your breathing. Dismiss any chatter that tries to start up in your head and just focus on your breathing for at least one minute. Of course, longer is better, but even one minute has a positive effect.

Here is a list of more vibration-raising activities you can rotate into your own daily routine (I regularly incorporate several of these into my day):

Singing (the louder the better)
Dancing
Listening to your 'fight song" very loudly (and singing along of course)
Yelling your affirmations/declarations excitedly
Getting yourself ready/clean/dressed/put together
Making your bed
Eating fruits and vegetables
Sway test your food before you eat it - if you fall forward, yes; if you fall backwards, no
Serving someone
Forgiving someone
Sending love energetically to someone
Uplifting music
Reading an inspiring book
Looking at your vision board
Listing 10 positive things about yourself on your mirror
Quick and easy home improvement projects
Playing with a pet
Watching funny animal videos

"IF YOU ALWAYS DO WHAT YOU'VE ALWAYS DONE, YOU'LL ALWAYS GET WHAT YOU'VE ALWAYS GOT.

—

HENRY FORD

Chapter 15

Troubleshooting: What To Do When Manifesting Doesn't Seem To Work

You are following the manifesting formula, have a vision board with your goal on it, and keeping your vibration up, but still no sign of your goal happening? There are a few things that could be happening.

First, check and see if your vibration is getting lowered by your words. Lots of things can lower your vibration, but the most common I have seen is language. How do you talk about your goal? How do you talk about yourself? How do you talk about other people?

Language is so much more important than most people realize. Your words are creating your reality, lifting or hurting other people, and telling your subconscious how you want to be treated.

There is a protective waiting period in place that keeps you from manifesting instantly. Imagine if you could instantly manifest when you are angry - especially on the freeway.

When we are triggered, we aren't thinking clearly and often have thoughts of revenge that would land us in prison if we followed through on them. But we don't actually follow through on them because we are good people and those passing angry thoughts only last for a second or two. If we could instantly manifest our desires, we could be in big trouble!

That is why we have that protective waiting period that slows down our ability to get what we want. It's like the waiting period required when trying to buy a gun - it's there to protect you from doing something stupid and irreversible.

I was taught this concept by Kirk Duncan, one of my mentors. He says the way to shorten your waiting period is to practice loving and forgiving yourself and others, and to especially control your negative thoughts and words. The more positive and loving you are to yourself and others, the shorter your waiting period becomes. So if you feel like your goal is taking way too long, check your language and adjust it to shorten your protective waiting period.

Second, check and see if you are letting other people play with your emotions. How many times have you been in a good mood and then someone you know says something or does something that sets you off? Why do you let them trigger you? How can you take back your power from them?

Boundaries are very important in maintaining your high vibration long enough to achieve your goal. Stop letting people trigger you, take advantage of you, and push your buttons. When you have a relationship like that, it would serve you well to either end the relationship or reshape it with better boundaries. It can be hard to stand your ground, but if your goal is worth enough to you, you will find the strength to do it. And if you can't, then that is a good thing to look at and do some breakthrough work on.

Third, check for subconscious programming that says you can't have what you want. Most people have this issue on some level, so I am going to teach you how to rewrite negative subconscious programming.

This technique is called belief breakthrough, and it is explained very thoroughly in a book written by my mentor Kris Krohn, *Limitless: Reclaim Your Power, Unleash Your Potential, Transform Your Life*. With Kris's permission, I am sharing the steps to a belief breakthrough here.

1. Get grounded. Uncross your arms and legs, sit comfortably with your eyes closed, and take 4 deep breaths. Imagine a light coming down from your higher power to the top of your head then all the way through you, out the bottoms of your feet, through the layers of the earth. Imagine it burning out all doubt, confusion, distraction, negativity, etc.

2. Ask yourself what limiting belief is holding you back right now.

3. Ask yourself what memory you need to see and resolve to work on replacing that limiting belief. See the perfect memory float up to your awareness, no matter how unrelated it may seem.

4. Identify the deeper limiting belief. Think about the emotions that you felt during that memory. Figure out what you decided about yourself in that moment when your young brain was trying to make sense of something it couldn't really understand.

5. Examine the cost of having that belief about yourself. Health, finances, relationships with others, relationship with yourself. Include past, present, and future costs.

6. Ask if you are ready to STOP paying that cost? Give yourself permission to stop paying that cost so you can choose a new belief that will serve you better.

7. Come up with a new belief that is productive and positive, that you can believe now, and claim it out loud with conviction.

8. Revisit the memory and either rewrite or reinterpret it with the help of a trusted advocate. They can be a real or imaginary person; past, present, or future, including God or even yourself at any point in time. Take the pain out of the memory and take the belief out of your operating system.

9. Celebrate the new memory or new interpretation of it with positive emotions and actions, either in the memory, or some time later today. This helps create a new neural pathway in your brain for the new belief.

10. Ask yourself what your next step is to make that new belief part of your core beliefs, then do that next step within 24 hours.

I recommend a daily belief breakthrough for all of my clients. Make it part of your morning routine and watch your life change for the better! I have used it regularly for three years now and I am amazed at the changes in my own core beliefs and how those changes have allowed me to reach so many more of my own goals.

Fourth, check and see if your goal is too big.

Sometimes we need to break our goals down into smaller goals, or baby steps. Outline all the steps you know are needed to reach your goal, then turn each one of those steps into a goal and start working only on the first one.

Success energy is powerful, so as you have small successes with the smaller steps of your goal, you will gain momentum and it will get easier to manifest the next small goal. If your goal is to make $10,000 each week, start with a smaller goal of $10,000 in a month. If your goal is to release 100 pounds, start with a smaller goal of releasing 1% of your current body weight. If your goal is to organize and de-clutter your house, start with a smaller goal of cleaning out and organizing your closet. Success breeds success, so make sure you have smaller goals to feed your brain successes.

Fifth, you need to meet more people. Reaching a goal frequently requires new connections in your life. If you've never reached a certain goal before, you probably need new information and resources that you didn't have before.

This requires meeting new people. Go to networking meetings, start a Meetup, attend events, and remember to ask to speak at events if you are a speaker. Grow your Facebook friends list, and sincerely message people that you are drawn to - not in a sales-driven energy.

Building your network of humans is one of the best ways to tap into new resources that will help you manifest that goal that seems impossible.

And finally, ask yourself if you are really doing the Drive-Thru Method properly. Are you cutting corners regularly? Are you procrastinating your action steps? Are you skipping steps entirely? Are you doing the manifesting formula daily?

When you perform the 6 steps faithfully, you can't help but get results. So always ask yourself if there is anything you can do to improve your performance of the formula.

The Drive-Thru Method of Manifesting

Now that you have several avenues for troubleshooting, you can explore any or all of them when you feel like manifesting isn't working for you. If you want a goal, that goal wants you. Don't try to talk yourself out of wanting to reach it when it's not showing up quickly enough for you.

Find the glitch in your thoughts, words, or actions so that you can fully commit to the manifesting formula every day and finally get the things you want.

REMEMBER TO CELEBRATE MILESTONES AS YOU PREPARE FOR THE ROAD AHEAD.

—

NELSON MANDELA

Chapter 16

What's Next?

This book has been created specifically to help you move out of 'hopeless, helpless, and stuck' into a place where you are reaching every goal you set and living the life of your dreams. I am not living the life of my dreams yet, because with every level-up, I create a new, bigger dream. I am definitely living the life of my dreams from three years ago.

But, just like me, you will reach your current goals and then look around and say, "Now what?"

There is a very important step you might miss if, when you reach your destination, you immediately start looking for the next one. And that important step is **celebrating your wins.**

You did it! You made this thing happen with your thoughts, words, actions, and Higher Power! Look at your progress! Take some time to enjoy it and revel in it! You are a creator of new realities!

Remember to give yourself credit for all your effort and hard work, and please journal about it too. Record your thoughts and feelings as you reach this moment where you bent reality to your will. Keep track of the things you manifest so that when you feel discouraged you can pull out your notes and read the account of you achieving a once-impossible goal. It will remind you of your power, your determination, your success, and your vision.

My story is just beginning. I will continue to fulfill my mission of teaching the world how to get everything they want instead of feeling hopeless, helpless, and stuck.

Your story is just beginning, too. You also have lives to touch and a world to change. Keep going. Keep making your dreams into your reality. Keep following your path to greatness.

Why? Because we all need you to be the best you can be. People are waiting for you to get up and start leading. It's time. You are ready.

Thank you for letting me be a tiny part of your journey.

And may you manifest miracles every day!

About the Author

Kelly Kaye Walker is an international speaker. She also coaches female entrepreneurs who are ready to align with their purpose, get out of their own way, and manifest the influence and impact for which they were born.

She has been married to her husband since 1996 and they have one son who loves improvising on the piano. She is the oldest of 4 kids and spent her school years in Kansas but has now lived in Utah for nearly 30 years.

After getting a bachelor's degree in art, she spent over 2 decades as a graphic designer before she found her true calling as a mentor and speaker in 2017. Kelly has a desire to learn more languages and loves to travel (frequently by cruise ship) with family, friends, and clients.

She has been known to carry on conversations with trees and loves to sit by the river having breakthroughs with her husband.

Connect with Kelly on Facebook by joining her free group: Manifesting Influence, Clients, and Purpose.

Check out her website at www.thequeenofmanifesting.com

Subscribe to her podcast, The Queen of Manifesting on iTunes, Amazon Music, Spotify and all other major podcast platforms.

www.ingramcontent.com/pod-product-compliance
Lightning Source LLC
Chambersburg PA
CBHW051400290426
44108CB00015B/2093